221 Amazing

MARINE ANIMALS

Encyclopedia

MANOJ PUBLICATIONS

221 Amazing Marine Animals Encyclopedia

Publishers:

MANOJ PUBLICATIONS

761, Main Road, Burari, Delhi-110084
Mobile : 09999476076, 9868112194,
　　　　　8178823569, 8178854810
Email　: info@manojpublications.com

For online shopping visit our website :
www.sawanonlinebookstore.com

ISBN : 978-81-310-2388-4

TERM USED	MEANING IN CONTEXT
Amphipod	Any of a large order (Amphipoda) of small crustaceans (as the sand flea) with a laterally compressed body
Anal fin	An unpaired fin on the underside of a fish behind the anus
Arthropod	An invertebrate animal such as insect, spider or crustacean
Barbells	A fleshy growth from the mouth or snout of a fish
Benthic	Occurring in the depths of the ocean
Byssal	Filaments secreted by some clams for attaching to hard surfaces
Cannibal	An organism that eats its own species
Caudal/tail fin	The fin at the end of a fish's body continuos with the tail
Cephalic	Pertaining to the head
Copepod	Crustaceans related to crabs, lobsters, etc.
Crustacean	Hard-shelled or crusted marine animal like lobsters, shrimps, crabs, etc.
Demersal	Marine habitat found at or near the bottom of the ocean
Diurnal	Active during the day
Dorsal	A single fin on the back of a fish or whale, e.g. the tall triangular hind of a shark or killer whale
Echinoderm	A common name given to the marine animals with distinguishing radial symmetry like starfish and sea urchins
Egg scatterers	Fish that scatter their adhesive or non-adhesive eggs to fall to the substrate, into plants, or float to the surface
Gamete	A male or female reproductive cell. Egg in a female and sperm in a male
Gestation period	The duration between fertilization and birth
Habitat	The naturally occurring environment in which the animal lives
Herbivore	Feeding only on plants
Hermaphrodite	Having both male and female sexual organs
Holothurian	Sea cucumber
Invertebrates	Creatures lacking backbones
IUCN	International Union for the Conservation of Nature and Natural Resources
Keratin	Fibrous protein which is part of nails, claws or shells of some creatures
Krill	Shrimp like crustacean
Mantle	The main body of a Mollusc containing the heart, stomach, intestines and sex organs
Metamorphosis	The process of transformation from an immature form to an adult form
Molluscs	Invertebrates such as snails and slugs
Monogamous	Bonding between male and female which exclusively mate with each other
Mouthbrooding	Carrying eggs and developing young in the mouth till they develop
Nocturnal	Active at night
Operculum	A lid or flap covering the gills
Oviparous	Producing young ones by laying eggs that hatch outside the body
Ovoviviparous	Eggs are fertilized and hatched inside the body of the organism
Pectoral	Fins on either side just behind the head corresponding to limbs of vertebrates
Pelvic	The pair of fins on the underside of fish that help control the direction
Plankton	Small microscopic organisms that drift or swim weakly like bacteria, diatoms, jellyfish, etc.
Proboscis	Refers to the mouth parts, nose or snout
Protogynous	A hermaphrodite whose female reproductive organs mature before male reproductive organs
Spawning	To release or deposit eggs
Villiform teeth	Thin and crowded teeth resembling the bristles of a brush
Viviparous	Giving birth to live young ones

CONTENTS

The World of Marine Animals

Marine animals are creatures that live in the ocean. With the oceans covering almost two-thirds of the Earth's surface, you can imagine the abundance of creatures that live inside them. From the beautiful coral reefs to the largest mammals on the Earth, they include some of the unusual, the most beautiful and many yet-to-be-discovered creatures of the world. This book tells you about these creatures that live in water. Marine animals are comprised of many groups of creatures such as :

- **Fish–**They are cold-blooded, have backbones, fins and gills. More than 32,000 different species are found. These include sharks, rayfish, etc.

- **Molluscs–**They are invertebrates such as squids, octopuses and cuttlefish.

- **Crustaceans–**They are creatures with exoskeletons and include crabs, lobsters, shrimps, krills and barnacles.

- **Plankton–**These are microscopic organisms that cannot swim and drift with the ocean current. Algae, bacteria and protists are some examples.

- **Mammals–**They are warm-blooded creatures that breathe air and include whales, dolphins, seals, etc.

More than 2,30,000 species of animals are found in the sea and many more are yet to be discovered.

How do we remember all these thousands of marine animals?

Well, we can't; but it doesn't hurt to try! So, we begin by a process scientists and naturalists (people who study nature) call 'classification'. This means we build categories in which we place marine animals, based on some common or similar traits they share.
So, this is how we do it :

- **Kingdom**
- **Phylum**
- **Class**

How to Read this Book

Common Name :
Galapagos Batfish

Native to : *South-East Pacific Oceans*
Region where it is found

Scientific Name :
Ogcocephalus darwini;
Name referred to by
scientists and
naturalists

Interesting Fact :
The lure on its head
secretes a chemical that
attracts the prey.
A fun fact for
you to remember

Family : *Ogcocephalidae;*
Like a unique surname

Conservation Status : *Least Concern;*
Tells you whether the animal is facing a risk to
life or not

Why is it important for you to read this book?

The Earth is teeming with life, as it has for millennia; however, look around you. Do you see dinosaurs and sloths? No! They are extinct and all we can do is imagine how they must have been when they were alive, based on their fossils and bones. Unfortunately, a number of marine animals you will read about in this book, are critically threatened or endangered; some are vulnerable. Who can help them survive? You can! How will you know which animal needs your help? Read the book!

Why should we save marine animals?

There is a fine balance of life on Earth; sadly, man's greed has upset this balance; we have cut more forests than Nature can afford; we have destroyed precious animal habitat shamefully, not mindful that we have left exposed and homeless hundreds of helpless creatures!

Can you really help animals stay alive and healthy?

Yes! Some of you, after reading this book, may choose to become zoologists, biologists, naturalists and scientists- your studies and research may contribute valuable information to the human race to save marine animals such as the Baleen Whale or the Giant Catfish! And yes, you could bring back the balance in favour of Mother Nature!

1. Abalone (Black)

Common name : Black Abalone
Scientific name : Haliotis cracherodii
Family : Haliotidae
Native to : Mexico and United States
Interesting fact : They can keep your aquarium clean as they feed on algae.
Conservation status : Critically Endangered

Abalones are a group of edible sea snails. Their ears-shaped shells have a dull exterior and an iridescent interior composed of nacre, that is found on pearls. This herbivore has broad muscular feet for clinging to rocks. The gestation period is 7-14 days and they live for 30 years. They are popular as food and are used in jewellery.

2. Achilles Tang

Common name : Red-spotted surgeonfish, Redtail surgeonfish, Redspot surgeonfish
Scientific name : Acanthurus achilles
Family : Acanthuridae
Native to : Pacific coral reefs of Hawaii and Pitcairn
Interesting fact : The scaly spikes on its back resemble a surgeon's scalpel, and so it's called a surgeonfish!
Conservation status : Least Concern

This beautiful tropical fish is black with striking orange and white lining along the fins and tail and a prominent teardrop shape on the caudal area. They sell like hotcakes in the aquarium trade. These open water, egg scatterers are difficult to breed in captivity. They have a life span of 7 years and feed on mostly benthic algae.

3. Acorn Worm

Common name : Tongue worms
Scientific name : Enteropneusta
Family : Enteropneusta
Interesting Fact : Its skin secretes a bromide compound that keeps bacteria and predators away.
Conservation status : Not Evaluated

True to its name, the worm-shaped marine invertebrate has 3 parts—an acorn-shaped proboscis, a short fleshy collar and a long trunk. They live in U-shaped sand and mud burrows of ocean floor. They feed on bacteria, diatoms and microalgae by ingesting the sand stuck to them (deposit feeding) and secrete coils of digested sediments called cast. They also do this with water through suspension feeding.

4. Australian Sea Lion

Common name : Hair seal, Counsellor seal
Scientific name : Neophoca cinerea
Family : Otariidae
Native to : Australia and Indian Oceans
Interesting fact : Excellent rock climbers
Conservation status : Endangered

Australian sea lions are 'pinnipeds', *i.e.* they use their fins as feet. They have different breeding seasons which range from 5 to 7 months. A male is known as a 'bull', a female is called a 'cow' and a young one is called a 'beach weaner'. Like elephants, there have been incidents of alloparenting, where orphaned pups are adopted by other members of the herd.

5. African Pompano

Common name : Pennant fish, Threadfin trevally, Cobblerfish, Cuban jack
Scientific name : Alectis ciliaris
Family : Carangidae
Native to : Tropical coasts around the world
Conservation status : Least Concern

This beautiful silvery, iridescent fish lives in depths of less than 100 metres feeding on crustaceans and small fish. Juveniles float with the ocean current. You can tell the fish from its concave shape of the head near the eyes. These fish grow 130 cm long and can weigh up to 22 kg. They are very popular in recreational fishing.

6. Albacore

Common name : Albacore tuna, Pigfish, White meat tuna, Chicken of the sea
Scientific name : Thunnus alalunga
Family : Scombridae
Native to : Tropical and temperate oceans of the world
Conservation status : Near Threatened

This species of tuna is the popular 'white meat tuna' available in the US. Its bullet-shaped body is designed for speed and is dark blue with shades of white ventrally. Its average length is 1.4 metres and it weighs up to 60 kg and life span is 12 years. These fish are open sea hunters feeding on cephalopods, fish, crustaceans and gelatinous organisms. Spawning is from November to February.

7. Ambon Scorpionfish

Common name : Ambon stingfish, Ambon
firefish, Hairy scorpionfish
Scientific name : Pteroidichthys amboinensis
Family : Scorpaenidae
Native to : Indian and Pacific Ocean
Conservation status : Not Evaluated
    This chameleon of the sea, that can camouflage, lives
in sand debris of the ocean floor at a depth of 10-50 metres.
It has a wide head with a large mouth and pectoral fins. It waits
for the prey and inhales it by surprise. These fish raise their poisonous spikes
on their backs, heads and around the eyes when threatened and can cause death.

8. Anchovy

Common name : Regan's anchovy,
Silverstripe anchovy
Scientific name : Anchoa argentivittata
Family : Engraulidae
Native to : Eastern Pacific Ocean
Interesting fact : The eggs are transparent and the yolk has a unique shape like a
sausage
Conservation status : Least Concern
    This small salt water fish, popular as food, is green with a silver stripe giving it a blue
reflection. They come in sizes ranging from 2 to 40 cm and there are as many as 144 different
species. The snout is blunt and sharp teeth line the jaws. They love to eat plankton and
new-born fish.

9. Angelfish (French)

Common name : French angelfish
Scientific name : Pomacanthidae
Family : Pomacanthidae
Native to : Atlantic, Indian and Western
Pacific Oceans
Interesting fact : All fish are born as
females and can switch sex when required.
Conservation status : Not Evaluated
    Marine angelfish love shallow coral reefs. Their bodies are flattened with
small mouths, large pectoral fins and rounded tail fins. Brightly coloured and patterned, they
vary in sizes from 15-60 cm. They eat the algae on the coral reef, small fish, shrimps and
prawns. Their eggs stick to the plankton till they hatch. Its lifespan is about 8-15 years.

10. Anglerfish

Common name : Monkfish, Goosefish
Scientific name : Lophiiformes
Family : Lophiidae
Native to : All oceans of the world
Interesting fact : The male does not attain
sexual maturity unless it attaches to the female,
leading a parasitic life thereafter.
Conservation status : Not Evaluated

Living in the deep, dark ocean floor is the angry ooking anglerfish with a huge head and a mouth that is lined with sharp teeth. Its unique light-emitting dangler on the head lures prey and attracts the tiny males who live life like parasites, attached to the females. They spawn between May and August. Average lifespan is about 20 years.

11. Anthias

Common name : Reeffish, Wreckfish, Jewelfish
Scientific name : Anthiinae
Family : Serranidae
Native to : Deep reefs in the tropical and sub-tropical
Atlantic
Interesting fact : All anthias are born females and
switch sex only when required.
Conservation status : Not Evaluated

This is one of the most beautiful groups of reeffish in the ocean found in a rainbow of colours. They move in groups of thousands called a 'shoal' which every deep-sea photographer has probably captured. As many as 200 species are known. They feed on zooplankton, crustacean larvae, fish eggs and small organisms that float in the water.

12. Atlantic Sea Raven

Common name : Bullhead, Puff-belly, Whippy, Sculpin
Scientific name : Hemitripterus americanus
Family : Hemitripteridae
Native to : New England and North-West Atlantic
Interesting fact : Their bellies inflate when
out of water and are unable to submerge
Conservation status : Not Evaluated

You'll find this large species of scorpion fish in rocky bottoms of the ocean at a depth of 180 metres. It can grow to a size of 18-20 inches and weigh up to 3.2 kg. This fish loves to eat crustaceans, molluscs, sea urchins, fish and bottom invertebrates. It uses sponge beds for spawning by attaching the eggs to its base.

13. Atlantic Wolf-fish

Common name : Sea wolf, Sea cat, Ocean catfish, Devil fish, Wolf eel
Scientific name : Anarhichas lupus
Family : Anarhichadidae
Native to : West and East coast of the Atlantic
Interesting fact : Its body contains a natural anti-freeze to thrive in a cold habitat.
Conservation status : Endangered

   This shy fish with an eel-like body has a dorsal fin running the whole length of the body. They grow to 1 metres in length and become blue as adults. Their strong jaws and molars grind away molluscs, crustaceans and echinoderms. Eggs are internally fertilized and guarded by the males when laid. Its skin is used as leather.

14. Australian Lungfish

Common name : Queensland lungfish, Burnett salmon, Barramunda
Scientific name : Neoceratodus forsteri
Family : Ceratodontidae
Native to : Queensland
Interesting fact : It has only one lung whereas other species have a pair and can live outside water for days.
Conservation status : Not Evaluated

   The only living member of the family, the Australian lungfish is a species as old as dinosaurs. Found in freshwater pools and rivers, they eat frogs, snails, earthworms and plants. Due to poor eyesight, they rely on electroreception to hunt for prey. They spawn at night from August to December; eggs hatch after three weeks.

15. Atlantic Guitarfish

Common name : Freckled guitarfish
Scientific Name : Rhinobatos lentiginosus
Family : Rhinobatidae
Native to : Western Atlantic Ocean
Interesting fact : It has no spine on its tail.
Conservation status : Near Threatened

   The Atlantic guitarfish looks like a hybrid between a shark and a ray. Its flat body is freckled with white spots, has well developed dorsal fins, triangular caudal fins and tapers to a thick tail, resembling a guitar in totality. These fish live in sandy coastal waters often close to coral reefs and feed on fish, benthic crustaceans and shellfish.

16. *Axilspot Hogfish*

Common name : Axil hogfish,
Coral hogfish, Panda hogfish
Scientific name : Bodianus axillaris
Family : Labridae
Native to : Indo-Pacific Ocean
Interesting fact : The body colour changes
drastically from juveniles to adults.
Conservation status : Least Concern

Axilspot hogfish inhabit lagoons and seaward reefs feeding on molluscs and crustaceans. Males are reddish-brown with a white posterior and large dark spots on the fins. Juveniles and females are black with a few white spots. Adults grow to a size of 20 cm. They exhibit distinct pairing during breeding and are oviparous. It is a popular aquarium fish.

17. *Axolotl*

Common name : Mexican walking fish, Mexican salamander
Scientific name : Ambystoma mexicanum
Family : Ambystomatidae
Native to : Mexico
Interesting fact : They can regenerate limbs,
kidneys, hearts and lungs, if damaged or lost.
Conservation status : Critically Endangered

The axolotl is actually an amphibian larva that
skips metamorphosis. Adults are gilled with huge
heads, lidless eyes and underdeveloped limbs. Three pairs of external gills behind the head are used to breathe, but this fish can also breathe through its skin. It feeds on worms, insects and small fish by suction. Its lifespan is about of 10 years.

18. *Azure Damsel*

Common name : Half-blue demoiselle, Yellow-dipped damsel
Scientific name : Chrysiptera hemicyanea
Family : Pomacentridae
Native to : Indo-Pacific and Eastern Indian Oceans,
especially in Indonesia and Western Australia
Interesting fact : Due to its vivid colouration and hardy
nature it is popular as a pet.
Conservation status : Not Evaluated

The azure damsel is a treat to the eyes with its blue
and yellow body. They live as a group in acropora corals
found in shallow waters. They form pairs for mating, following which the males prepare the coral for females to deposit their sticky eggs and guard them aggressively till they hatch. Plankton make up their diet.

19. Baleen Whale

Common name : Whalebone whale
Scientific name : Mysticeti
Native to : Oceans worldwide
Interesting fact : They use sound for communication and are known to 'sing' during breeding season.
Conservation status : Endangered

Baleen whales, a group of 15 species, including one of the largest animals, the blue whale, feed on the smallest fish like krill by filter feeding. They do this with baleen plates made of keratin, that hang like bristles from their upper jaws. Other favourites are herring, pollack and plankton. Two blowholes keep the water away when they breathe.

20. Banggai Cardinalfish

Common name : Kaudern's cardinal, Longfin cardinalfish
Scientific name : Pterapogon kauderni
Family : Apogonidae
Native to : Banggai Islands of Indonesia
Interesting fact : Adult males keep the young in their mouths after hatching for an undetermined period.
Conservation status : Endangered

Found among coral reefs, sea urchins, sea anemones and mangrove roots are these tiny tropical marine fish. It has a silver body with three black bars across the head and body and tasselled dorsal fins. Caudal fins are elongated. Found in groups of 9, it feeds on planktonic, demersal and benthic organisms. Its lifespan is 1-2 years.

21. Barnacle

Scientifc name : Cirripedia
Family : Thecostraca
Native to : Found worldwide
Interesting fact : Most barnacles are hermaphroditic producing both male and female reproductive cells and reproduce sexually.
Conservation status : Least Concern

The barnacle is a marine arthropod living in shallow and tidal waters. There are 1,220 species of the barnacle currently known. They hardly move and live attached to boats, rocks, turtles and whales. Some live within crabs. The shell, made of six plates, has feathery legs that draw water for filter feeding of plankton and microscopic plants and animals.

22. Barracuda

Common name : California barracuda, Pacific barracuda, Pacific barracuda
Scientific name : Sphyraena argentea
Family : Sphyraenidae
Native to : Oceans worldwide
Interesting fact : The age of a barracuda can be determined by counting the rings on its scales and the inner ear.
Conservation status : Least Concern

This large, fearsome, solitary fish thrives in tropical and sub-tropical oceans. It has a shiny, long body covered in smooth scales. Their sharp fang-like teeth help them grip their food such as jacks, groupers, snappers, small tunas, mullets, herrings and anchovies. They breed in spring spawning in deeper waters. Its lifespan is about 14 years.

23. Barrel-eye Fish

Common name : Spook fish
Scientific name : Macropinna microstoma
Family : Opisthoproctidae
Native to : North Pacific Ocean
Interesting fact : The structures mistaken for their eyes actually do the job of a nose.
Conservation status : Not Evaluated

With an apt common name, the spook fish has barrel-shaped eyes set inside a transparent head. They can hence look upward to detect the silhouettes of prey. They can even rotate their eyes. Its dark body is covered in silvery scales and a small mouth ends in a snout. It feeds on small zooplankton like hydroids, copepods and other crustaceans.

24. Basket Star

Common name : Brittle star
Scientific name : Euryalina
Family : Euryalidae
Native to : Oceans worldwide
Interesting fact : Basket stars can grow back their limbs if damaged or lost during hunting.
Conservation status : Not Evaluated

Living in the deep waters of the world are these tree-like, marine invertebrates of the order Euryalida with about 177 species. Their arms branch out repeatedly almost growing to 70 cm long. They can weigh up to 5 kg. The arms have little hooks for capturing zooplankton for food. They breathe by pumping water into their systems, feeding and excreting through their mouths. They reproduce both sexually and asexually. Its lifespan is 35 years.

25. *Bat Ray*

Common name : Eagle ray
Scientific name : Myliobatis californicus
Family : Myliobatidae
Native to : Pacific Ocean
Interesting fact : They expose prey buried in the sand by flapping their wings and can dig up to 13 feet using their snouts.
Conservation status : Least Concern

Bat rays, closely related to sharks, love estuaries and bays, kelp beds and rocky bottoms of shallow shores. Their bat-like wings can be 6 feet wide and they weigh 91 kg. Though calm, they sting with their venomous spines in their tails when attacked. Their teeth, fused into plates, can crush molluscs, crustaceans and small fish. Their lifespan is 23 years.

26. *Bearded Seal*

Common name : Square flipper seal
Scientific name : Erignathus barbatus
Family : Phocidae
Native to : Arctic Ocean
Interesting fact : They create breathing holes by pushing with their heads, to breathe while under ice.
Conservation status : Least Concern

Aptly named, these ice-loving seals have whiskers resembling a beard. This greyish-brown creature has no ears. It can grow to a length of 2.1 to 2.7 metres and weigh 200-430 kg. Crustaceans, molluscs, sculpin, flatfish and cod make up their diet. Pups are born in spring on small drifting ice floes and enter water a few hours later.

27. *Beluga Whale*

Common name : White whale, Sea canary, Melon head
Scientific name : Delphinapterus leucas
Family : Monodontidae
Native to : Arctic and sub-Arctic regions
Interesting fact : They can swim backwards and change the shape of their foreheads by blowing air into them.
Conservation status : Near Threatened

Mimicking the ice around them, beluga whales are white in colour with globular heads. It can grow up to 5.5 metres in length and weigh up to 1,600 kg. A layer of fat covers the whole body for insulation and helps during starvation. Its diet includes fish, crustaceans and deep sea invertebrates. Its lifespan is 70-80 years.

28. Black Banded Cat Shark

Common name : Brown banded bamboo shark, Cat shark
Scientific name : Chiloscyllium punctatum
Family : Hemiscyllidae
Native to : Western Pacific
Ocean and Indian Ocean
Interesting fact : It can survive
out of water for about 12 hours.
Conservation status : Near Threatened

    True to its name, the cat shark has whisker-like barbells near its mouth for sensing prey. Juveniles have black bands on their bodies. This fish has leg-like muscular pectoral and pelvic fins enabling it to live in reefs and crevices. This solitary and nocturnal animal feeds on crabs, shrimps and small fish. Eggs are laid on the sea bed. Its lifespan is 20 years.

29. Blob Sculpin

Scientific name : Psychrolutes phrictus
Family : Psychrolutidae
Native to : North Pacific Ocean by the
coasts of Japan, the Bering Sea and California
Interesting fact : The fish collapses into a
jelly-like blob when taken out of the water.
Conservation status : Not Evaluated

    Living in the deep sea is this spiky, grey colour fish
with a huge head. It grows to a maximum size of 70 cm and weighs
up to 9.5 kg. It is a sedentary animal feeding mostly on crustaceans, molluscs and sea urchins. Males guard the eggs laid by females. Their lifespan is 3-6 years.

30. Blue Crab

Common name : Chesapeake blue crab, Atlantic blue crab
Scientific name : Callinectes sapidus
Family : Portunidae
Native to : Western Atlantic Ocean and the Gulf of Mexico
Interesting fact : Its scientific name means beautiful
savoury swimmer.
Conservation status : Vulnerable

    This ten-legged crustacean is found in brackish coastal
lagoons and estuaries. Its shell colour is blue to olive
with bright blue claws band red tips on females. Its fifth pair of legs are paddle-like making it a good swimmer. These fish feed on mussels, snails, fish, plants and smaller blue crabs. Mating is from May to October. Their lifespan is less than 3 years.

31. Blue-ringed Octopus

Scientifc name : Hapalochlaena
Family : Octopodidae
Native to : Pacific and Indian Oceans
Interesting fact : Females incubate eggs under their arms for 6 months and die after the eggs have hatched.
Conservation status : Not Evaluated

This highly photographed underwater creature is also the world's most venomous animal. They have yellowish skins and 50-60 blue and black rings covering the dorsal and lateral surfaces that darken when agitated. They have 8 arms which can be regenerated within six weeks. They feed on small crabs and shrimps. Their lifespan is 2 years.

32. Blue Whale

Common name : Sulphur bottom whale, Sibbald's rorqual
Scientific name: Balaenoptera musculus
Family : Balaenopteridae
Native to : Cold and temperate oceans of the world
Interesting fact : When these exhale through their blowholes, the water can reach a height of 30 feet.
Conservation status : Endangered

The blue whale is the largest living animal with a heart as big as a car. Its bluish-grey body is 30 metres long and weighs 170 tonnes. They eat some of the smallest creatures such as crustaceans or krill and copepods. They can hear one another even 1,600 km away. Breeding once in 3 years, they live for 80-90 years.

33. Bluefin Tuna (Southern)

Common name : Southern bluefin tuna
Scientific name : Thunnus maccoyii
Family : Scombridae
Native to : Argentina, Australia, Brazil, Indonesia, Madagascar, New Zealand and South Africa
Interesting fact : Bluefin Tuna has a nickname–Tunny.
Conservation status : Critically Endangered

The bluefin tuna, the largest of the tunas, is prized for sushi and has 3 species : Atlantic (Thannus thynnus), Pacific (Thannus orientalis) and Southern (Thannus maccoyii). They can swim up to 60 metres per hour and can dive more than 4,000 feet. They hunt by sight feeding on fish like herring, mackerel and even eels. Their lifespan is 33 years.

34. Box Jellyfish

Common name : Sea wasp,
Marine stingers
Scientific name : Chironex fleckeri
Family : Chirodropidae
Native to : Tropical and sub-tropical
oceans of the world
Interesting fact : Sea turtles, predators of the jellyfish, are not affected by sting.
Conservation status : Not Evaluated

The box jellyfish is one of the deadliest jellyfish. Its body is a transparent, cube-shaped bell with up to 15 tentacles. It has 4 true eyes for vision and 20 simple eyes for light detection. Its diet is made of small fish, prawns and bait fish. They mate once a year and die shortly after spawning. Their lifespan is less than a year.

35. Bull Shark

Common name : River Ganges shark, Zambezi
shark, Nicaragua shark
Scientific name : Carcharhinus leucas
Family : Carcharhinidae
Native to : Atlantic and Indian Oceans
Interesting fact : It is nicknamed as the
'pit bull of the sea' due to its aggressive behaviour.
Conservation status : Near Threatened

Lining the tropical coasts are these large, aggressive sharks with an average length of 2.4 metres, weighing 130 kg. This solitary hunter head-butts its prey like a bull before killing it. They eat almost anything from fish, dolphins to smaller sharks. It mates from late summer to early autumn. Gestation period is 12 months. They live for 16 years.

36. Canary Rockfish

Common name : Red snapper, Orange
rockfish, Fantail
Scientific name : Sebastes pinniger
Family : Sebastidae
Native to : Pacific coast
Interesting fact : They live really long life with a
lifespan of 75 years.
Conservation status : Critically Endangered

The canary rockfish is a brilliant orange-red fish living in rocky bottoms. Juveniles, however, enjoy shallow waters near rocky reefs and piers. Average length is 76 cm and they weigh up to 4 kg. Adults feed on demersal invertebrates and small fish, while juveniles feed on krill larvae, copepods and amphipods. It matures at about 5-6 years of age.

37. Candlefish

Common name : Eulachon, Hooligan, Oolichan, Ooligan
Scientific name : Thaleichthys pacificus
Family : Osmeridae
Native to : Pacific coast of
North America
Interesting fact : Due to its high
fat-content, it can burn like a candle when dried.
Conservation status : Least Concern

The candlefish is blue to brown on the back and the top of the head and silvery-white on the sides. It can grow 15-20 cm in length. Feeding on plankton, fish eggs, insect larvae and small crustaceans, it lives in oceans but returns to rivers and freshwater streams to spawn and die. Their lifespan is 5 years.

38. Chambered Nautilus

Common name : Nautilus, Pearly nautilus
Scientific name : Nautilus pompilius
Family : Nautilidae
Native to : Pacific and Indian Oceans
Interesting fact : Its beautiful shell is popular in
the shell trade and was used to make attractive
'Nautilus shell cups'.
Conservation status : Not Evaluated

This living fossil has brown zebra stripes on its smooth white shell, whose inside is coated with nacre, found on pearls. Internal chambers are added as they grow. Spilling out of the shell are 90 tentacles and a large eye. They live in deep, dark waters feeding on hermit crabs, fish and exoskeletons of crustaceans. Their lifespan is 15 years.

39. Chimaera Fish

Common name : Rabbitfish
Scientific name : Chimaera monstrosa
Family : Chimaeridae
Native to : Oceans worldwide
Interesting fact : Chimaeras are sold
as food in some regions of the world.
Conservation status : Near Threatened

Chimaeras are cartilaginous fish with 38 species, found in depths of 2500 metres or more. They are black to brownish-grey with elongated bodies and bulky heads with a single gill opening. A venomous spine in front of the dorsal fin is used in defence. It feeds on small fish and invertebrates. Eggs are laid in spindle-shaped, leathery cases.

40. Christmas Tree Worm

Common name : Jewel stone
Scientific name : Spirobranchus giganteus
Family : Serpulidae
Native to : Tropical oceans worldwide
Interesting fact : The plumes are quickly
retracted even when slightly disturbed.
Conservation status : Least Concern

   Christmas tree worms live embedded on corals, and come
in many colours. They are tube-dwelling worms with two cone-shaped
spiralling plumes used in feeding and respiration. It has well-developed digestive,
circulatory and nervous systems with a central brain. It feeds on plankton and suspended
food particles by filter feeding. Eggs and sperms are released into the water.

41. Cleaner Wrasse

Common name : Bluestreak cleaner
wrasse, Striped cleaner wrasse
Scientific name : Labroides dimidiatus
Family : Labridae
Native to : Indo-Pacific Ocean
Interesting fact : Cleaner wrasses are
hermaphrodites and can change sex when required.
Conservation status : Least Concern

   True to its name, the cleaner wrasse cleans unwanted parasites and dead tissues on
other reef fish. It sets up cleaning stations for other fish to visit. It has a lateral stripe along
the length of its body and has a dance-like move to identify itself to bigger fish. Its
lifespan in captivity is 4 years.

42. Clown Frogfish

Common name : Warty frogfish
Scientific name : Antennarius maculatus
Family : Antennariidae
Native to : Indo-Pacific Ocean
Conservation status : Not Evaluated

   The clown frogfish easily blends into its rocky, coral
environment with its colourful patterns and the ability to
camouflage. Growing up to 15 cm long, it has a globulous,
extensible body with the skin covered in warts. Its large mouth
can accommodate prey of its own size and it attacks all fish. It leads
a solitary lifestyle and reproduces oviparously.

43. Clown Trigger Fish

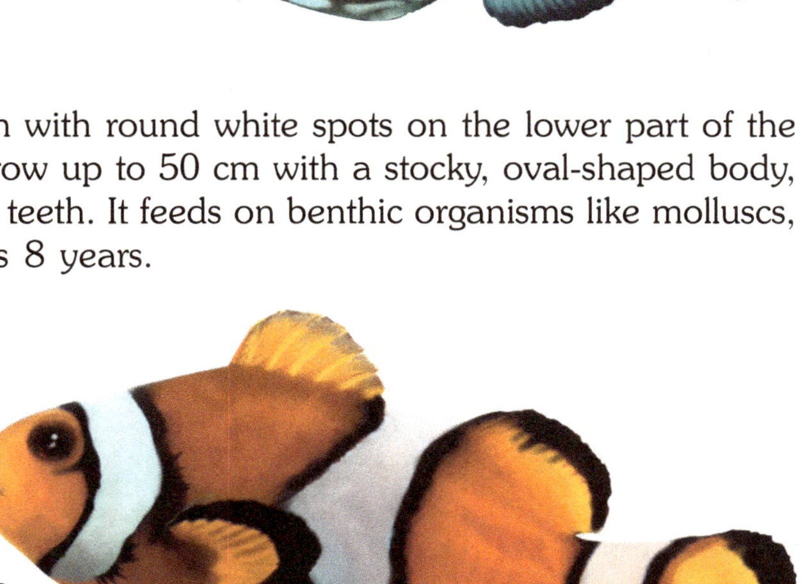

Common name : Bigspotted triggerfish
Scientific name : Balistoides conspicillum
Family : Balistidae
Native to : Indo-Pacific Ocean
Interesting fact : A trigger-like spine in front of the dorsal fin helps the fish wedge itself into crevices.
Conservation status : Not Evaluated

The clown triggerfish is a small black fish with round white spots on the lower part of the body. It is a diurnal, solitary fish that can grow up to 50 cm with a stocky, oval-shaped body, a large head and a small mouth with strong teeth. It feeds on benthic organisms like molluscs, echinoderms and crustaceans. Its lifespan is 8 years.

44. Clown Fish

Common name : Orange clown fish
Scientific name : Amphiprion percula
Family : Pomacentridae
Native to : Indo-Pacific Ocean
Interesting fact : Clown fish are all born as males and switch sex only when required.
Conservation status : Endangered

The clown fish, popularized by the movie (Finding Nemo), is found in tropical coral reefs. It grows 10-18 cm and is orange, yellow, red or blackish with white bars or patches. They never get stung by sea anemones, with whom they live, protecting them from predators and parasites, getting food in return. Their lifespan is 6-10 years.

45. Cod (Atlantic)

Common name : Atlantic cod, Codling, Haberdine, Kil'din cod
Scientific name : Gadus morhua
Family : Gadidae
Native to : Atlantic Ocean
Interesting fact : Cod liver oil is extracted from cods for its vitamins and omega-3 fatty acids.
Conservation status : Vulnerable

Two popular species of cods are the Atlantic cod (Gadus morhua) and the Pacific cod (Gadus macrocephalus). It weighs an average of 5-12 kg. Being an active hunter, it feeds on sand eels, whiting, haddock, small cod, squids, crabs, lobsters, mussels, worms, mackerel and molluscs. It is enjoyed as food making humans its only predators. Its lifespan is 20 years.

46. Coelacanth

Common name : West Indian Ocean coelacanth, African coelacanth, Gombessa
Scientific name : Latimeria chalumnae
Family : Latimeriidae
Native to : Atlantic and Indian Ocean
Interesting fact : Coelacanths have electricity detecting organs in their snouts.
Conservation status : Critically Endangered

Coelacanth means 'hollow spine' in Greek, referring to its hollow fin spines. It is a large fish growing up to 1.8 metres and weighing up to 90 kg. It has unique lobed fins that move like legs. Its skull has a hinged joint for eating large prey. It feeds on cuttlefish, squids and octopuses. Lifespan is 60 years.

47. Conch

Scientific name : Strombus gigas
Family : Strombidae
Native to : Indian and Pacific Oceans
Interesting fact : The meat of a conch is edible and its shells are used as souvenirs and musical instruments.

A conch is a group of sea snails of about 50 species. They inhabit sandy bottoms among the bed of sea grass in tropical waters. Their spiral shells are right-handed and come in white, brown, orange and pink colours. They feed on algae. Eggs are laid in long, twisted gelatinous tubes. Their lifespan is 20-30 years.

48. Copepod

Common name : Plankton
Scientific name : Copepoda
Native to : Oceans and freshwater worldwide
Interesting fact : The cysts produced by females can remain dormant for years and hatch when returned to water.

Copepods are the most abundant creatures living in water with over 13,000 known species. These small crustaceans are 1-2 mm long with teardrop shaped bodies, large antennae and armoured exoskeletons. With no gills, oxygen is directly absorbed into their bodies. They clean the water they live in by feeding on phytoplankton, organic detritus and the bacteria growing on them. They reproduce both by mating and by females producing cysts.

49. *Coral*

Scientific name : Anthozoa
Family : Alcyonacea
Native to : Oceans worldwide
Interesting fact : The Great Barrier reef in Australia is the largest coral reef that is 2600 km long.
Conservation status : Threatened

Corals are invertebrate animals that look like plants. Over 70,000 species of corals are known. They grow in clear, shallow waters with good sunlight. Each coral is called a polyp, which attaches to a rock, multiplies and forms colonies or reefs. Though translucent yet their colours are due to the algae that grow on them. They also have tentacles to feed on plankton, fish and shrimp. Reproduction is asexual. Lifespan is 15-30 years.

50. *Cortez Rainbow Wrasse*

Common name : Paddlefin wrasse, Mexican rainbow wrasse, Lollipop wrasse
Scientific name : Thalassoma lucasanum
Family : Labridae
Native to : Eastern Pacific Ocean
Conservation status : Least Concern

Found in the Sea of Cortez, these beautifully coloured fish live in small groups in reefs. Females and males have yellow, red and blue-green stripes running along their bodies while some terminal, females (that become males) have blue head and broad yellow bars behind them. This fish feeds on crustaceans, algae, eggs of fish and sea urchins. Juveniles clean parasites from larger fish.

51. *Crocodile Fish*

Common name : De Beaufort's flathead, Giant flathead
Scientific Name : Cymbacephalus beauforti
Family : Platycephalidae
Native to : Western Pacific Oceans
Interesting fact : Their eyes have frilly lappets to camouflage their irises effectively.
Conservation status : Not Evaluated

Aptly named, this fish looks like a crocodile with its flat head and a long body which is mottled for camouflage. They are found in mangroves, seagrass or coral reefs at depths up to 30 metres. It can grow up to 50 cm, the average being 35 cm. It feeds on small fish and crustaceans. Its lifespan is 2 years.

52. Crown of Thorns

Common name : Crown of thorns starfish
Scientific name : Acanthaster planci
Family : Acanthasteridae
Native to : Indo-Pacific Ocean
Interesting fact : The stomach of this starfish secretes digestive enzymes to absorb nutrients from liquefied coral.
Conservation status : Not Evaluated

The crown of thorns is a starfish with many arms and venomous spines covering its surface. It is one of the largest sea stars growing up to 25-35 cm with up to 21 arms. Its unique diet is made of hard reef coral polyps. Breeding in early to mid-summer, it reproduces by spawning, releasing gametes into the sea water. Its lifespan is 16 years.

53. Dana Octopus Squid

Scientific name : Taningia danae
Family : Octopoteuthidae
Native to : North Atlantic Ocean, Cape Verde Islands
Interesting fact : During mating, the male cuts the female's flesh to deposit its sperms.
Conservation status : Least Concern

One of the largest known squids, they grow 1.7-2.3 metres long and weigh up to 161.4 kg. The bioluminescent photophores on its arm emit blinding flashes of light to confuse its prey and escape from predators. Prey such as fish, crabs and molluscs are grabbed with the claws on its suckers. Their lifespan is less than a year.

54. Delta Smelt

Scientifc name : Hypomesus transpacificus
Family : Osmeridae
Native to : Sacramento–San Joaquin River Delta in California
Interesting fact : The delta smelts die shortly after spawning.
Conservation status : Critically Endangered

Found only in California, the delta smelt is a tiny, transparent, silvery blue fish found in the freshwater-saltwater mixing zone of the estuary but migrates to freshwater for spawning. It is pelagic and can tolerate a wide range of salinity. It feeds on plankton, copepods, amphipods, insects' larvae and opossum shrimp. Lifespan is only one year.

55. Dogface Puffer Fish

Common name : Black-spotted puffer
Scientific name : Arothron nigropunctatus
Family : Tetraodontidae
Native to : Indian and Pacific Oceans
Interesting fact : The skin of this
puffer fish secretes mucus to protect
itself from parasites.
Conservation status : Least Concern

    This puffer fish has unique canine features giving it the common name. It holds a deadly poison and can inflate its body by swallowing air or water to ward off enemies. From grey to light brown, blue, yellow and orange, it changes body colour during its different phases. This solitary creature feeds on benthic invertebrates, sponges, algae, coral, crustaceans and molluscs.

56. Dolphin

Common name : Heaviside's dolphin,
Benguela dolphin
Scientific name : Cephalorhynchus heavisidii
Family : Delphinidae
Native to : Angola, Namibia and South Africa
Interesting fact : Being mammals, dolphins are born with hair on top of the
rostrum which is lost after two weeks.
Conservation status : Data Deficient

    Dolphins are playful mammals living in water, closely related to whales. With more than forty species, they come in sizes from 1.2-9.5 metres long and can weigh 80-235 kg. Its body is streamlined and rounded with a dark back and a white belly. The pectoral flippers are similar to the forelimbs of land animals. They breathe through blowholes on top of their heads and use echolocation to find prey such as squids, fish, shrimps and crustaceans.

57. Dottyback

Common name : Forktail dottyback
Scientific name : Pseudochromis dixurus
Family : Pseudochromidae
Native to : Egypt, Israel, Jordan, Saudi Arabia,
Sudan and India
Interesting fact : Males guard the fertilized eggs and fan
them to provide oxygen, not letting even females near them.
Conservation status : Least Concern

    Dottybacks are small, vividly coloured reef fish with about 120 known species. They are 2-10 cm in length and have 3 or less spines in the dorsal fin. Crustaceans, zooplankton, polychaetes and small fish make up their diet. All dottybacks are hermaphrodites, capable of switching their sex. They are hardy aquarium fish with a lifespan of 5-7 years.

58. Dragon Moray Eel

Common name : Dragon eel, Dragon moray, Hawaiian dragon eel, Leopard moray eel
Scientific name : Enchelycore pardalis
Family : Muraenidae
Native to : Indo-Pacific region
Interesting fact : The eel changes colour and pattern as its matures into an adult.
Conservation status : Not Evaluated

The dragon moray eel is a stunning orange fish with white and brown spots like those of a leopard. These aggressive predators have sharp-pointed heads and horns above the eyes, earning them their name. The mouth has sharp teeth and a curved lower jaw that cannot close. They feed on small fish, crabs, shrimps and squids.

59. Dragonet (Sailfin)

Common name : Sailfin Dragonet
Scientific name : Callionymus pusillus
Family : Callionymidae
Native to : Atlantic, Mediterranean and Black Sea
Conservation status : Least Concern

Dragonets are a group of colourful fish, with 139 species, living in sandy bottoms of the ocean. They have elongated, scaleless bodies, flat triangular heads with large mouths and eyes and fan-shaped, tapering tail fins. Males and females are coloured and patterned differently. Copepods, amphipods, worms, crustaceans and small invertebrates make up their diet. Their lifespan is 10-15 years.

60. Drift Fish

Common name : Fork tail, Indian ariomma, Indian drift fish
Scientific name : Ariomma indicum
Family : Ariommatidae
Native to : Indo-Pacific Oceans
Conservation status : Not Evaluated

Drift fish are small-to-medium fish with compressed slender bodies, about 1 metres long. They have large heads, blunt noses, small terminal mouths, two distinct dorsal fins and deeply forked caudal fins. They are uniformly coloured with darker blotches or stripes. Juveniles and larvae are often found living among jellyfish and siphonphores.

61. Dugong

Common name : Sea pig, Sea camel
Scientific name : Dugong dugon
Family : Dugongidae
Native to : Indo-Pacific Ocean
Interesting fact : A female gives birth in shallow water to just one calf after a gestation period of 13-15 months.
Conservation status : Vulnerable

Dugongs are elephant-like, large marine mammals found in shallow bays and mangroves. They grow up to 3 metres long. They have paddle-like forelimbs, dolphin-like tails and unique skull and teeth. They graze benthic sea grasses with their sharp downturned snouts. These herbivores occasionally eat jellyfish, sea squirts and shellfish. They hunted for their meat and oil. Their lifespan is 70 years.

62. Dungeness Crab

Common name : Cancer magister
Scientific name : Metacarcinus magister
Family : Cancridae
Native to : West coast of America
Interesting fact : It is named after a place called Dungeness in Washington, where it is found in abundance.
Conservation status : Not Evaluated

Dungeness crabs live in eelgrass beds and water bottoms and are popular as food due to their sweet taste and tender flesh. They molt their wide shells periodically to grow and have five pairs of legs. Its stomach has tooth-like structures to digest clams, crustaceans and small fish. If threatened, they bury themselves in the sand. Lifespan is 8-13 years.

63. Eastern Fiddler Ray

Common name : Banjo shark
Scientific name : Trygonorrhina fasciata
Family : Rhinobatidae
Native to : Australia
Conservation status : Least Concern

The eastern fiddler ray is a guitarfish found in shallow coastal sandy bays, seagrass beds and rocky reefs. They are brown with shades of yellow or olive and distinctive triangular patterns behind their eyes. A row of thorn-like denticles lines its back. They feed on shellfish, crabs and worms. They are ovoviviparous with a gestation period of 4-5 months. Their lifespan is 30 years.

64. *Electric Eel*

Scientific name : Electrophorus electricus
Family : Gymnotidae
Native to : Worldwide Oceans
Interesting fact : Electric eels have cells called electrocytes that produce electricity.

Conservation status : Least Concern

These are about 800 species of this snake-like fish living in the shallow waters of the ocean. Some are found deeper and others live in freshwater. With slimy bodies and reduced fins, they wriggle in mud and crevices. They are nocturnal, feeding on small fish, crustaceans and worms. Their lifecycle begins in the ocean, heading to rivers to spend their life and heading back to the ocean to spawn and die. Their lifespan is 20 years.

65. *Elegant Firefish*

Common name : Purple firefish
Scientific name : Nemateleotris decora
Family : Microdesmidae
Native to : Indo-West Pacific region
Interesting fact : Elegant firefish are highly monogamous with couples building a nest and taking turns guarding it.

Conservation status : Not Evaluated

Living among reefs, sandy patches and rubble is this slender, colourful fish with a purple head and a white or yellow body that darkens to grey towards the tail. The fins have bands of purple, red, black and orange. It feeds on copepods, zooplankton and crustaceans, and quickly leaps into holes when disturbed. Lifespan is 3 years.

66. *Elephant Seal (Northern)*

Common name : Northern elephant seal
Scientific name : Mirounga angustirostris
Family : Phocidae
Interesting fact : Elephant seals can hold their breath under water for up to 2 hours.
Conservation status : Least concern

The elephant seal has a trunk-like proboscis (that of an elephant) that can produce loud noises. There are two types–the Northern elephant seal and the Southern elephant seal. Living in warm coastal zaters are these 16 feet long mammals that weigh up to 3,000 kg. It feeds on skates, rays, squids, octopuses, eels, small sharks and large fish. Lifespan is 14-22 years.

67. Elephant Snail

Common name : Roman shield
Scientific name : Scutus antipodes
Family : Fissurellidae
Native to : Australia
Interesting fact : Elephant snails have a well-developed sense of light and can tell light and shade apart.
Conservation status : Not Evaluated

The elephant snail looks like someone stepped on it. Its jet-black body has an oval-shaped, dirty-white shell, concealed under the skin folds of its mantle which it exposes when threatened. They live under rocks and boulders at low tide level. They come out in the night to avoid drying of the mantle and to feed on algae in pools, crevices or under stones.

68. Emperor Shrimp

Common name : Imperial cleaner shrimp, Emperor partner shrimp
Scientific name : Periclimenes imperator
Family : Palaemonidae
Native to : Indo-Pacific region
Interesting fact : The emperor shrimp will perform a manicure if a diver happens to put his hand near it.
Conservation status : Not Evaluated

You can find emperor shrimps hanging upside down, on nudibrachs, holothurians, sea slugs and sea cucumbers with which they form commensalistic relationships. Its red body has white lines and purple-tipped claws. These 1.9 cm long creatures eat up the host's ectoparasites while the host gives them protection. They also feed on algae and plankton.

69. Epaulette Shark

Common name : Carpet shark, Cat shark, Blind shark, Walking shark
Scientific name : Hemiscyllium ocellatum
Family : Hemiscylliidae
Native to : Australia and New Guinea
Interesting fact : To cope with oxygen depletion during night, the shark increases the blood supply to its brain by shutting down non-essential neural functions.
Conservation status : Least Concern

Living in shallow waters of tidal pools, coral flats and staghorn corals is the epaulette shark. It is 70-90 cm long with a slender body, a short head and broad paddle-shaped fins. The body is light brown with dark spots and a large spot behind the pectoral fin. This nocturnal shark feeds on benthic invertebrates and small bony fish.

70. European Lobster

Common name : Common lobster, Clawed lobster
Scientific name : Homarus gammarus
Family : Nephropidae
Native to : Widespread in North-East Atlantic, Mediterranean and Black Sea
Interesting fact : They can swim backwards using their soft and flexible tails.
Conservation status : Least Concern

The European lobster has an asymmetrical pair of pincers with one for cutting and the other for crushing prey. They live in holes of coral and rocky reefs. The outer hard shell is shed several times for growth. This blue-coloured lobster turns red on cooking. It feeds on crabs, molluscs, urchins, starfish and worms. Its lifespan is 40 years.

71. False Killer Whale

Scientific name : Pseudorca crassidens
Family : Delphinidae
Native to : Temperate and Tropical waters worldwide
Interesting fact : The scientific name 'crassidens' of the false killer whale means 'thick-tooth' referring to its fearsome conical teeth.
Conservation status : Data Deficient

False killer whales are huge growing 5-6 metres long and weighing 1200-2200 kg. Its slender body is black with a grey neck, has an elongated tapered head, a sickle-shaped dorsal fin and short pointed flippers. They travel in groups of 10-20 and are co-operative hunters, sharing the prey. They eat squid, tuna, mahimahi, threadfin jack and broadbill swordfish.

72. Fan Worm

Common name : European fan worm, Feather duster worm, Mediterranean fan worm
Scientific name : Sabella spallanzanii
Family : Sabellidae
Native to : East Atlantic and Mediterranean
Interesting fact : When threatened, its crown is withdrawn into the tube.
Conservation status : Not Evaluated

Fan worms live in shallow waters attached to rocks, concrete, boat hulls, mussels and oysters. They are segmented worms encased in a leathery tube with a crown of tentacles, that give them their common name. These filter feeders are white to light tan in colour, sometimes pink, light blue or other colour. Its lifespan is up to one year.

73. Fangtooth Fish

Common name : Common sabertooth, Common fangtooth
Scientific name : Anoplogaster cornuta
Family : Anoplogastridae
Native to : Oceans worldwide
Interesting fact : Despite its looks, the fangtooth fish is actually harmless and its scientific name 'Anoplo' means unarmed.
Conservation status : Not Evaluated

Living really deep in the sea, up to 5000 metres, is the dreadful-looking fangtooth fish. Growing up to 9 cm, they have big mouths that they can't shut due to their large fang-shaped teeth. They come to the surface during night and use contact chemoreception to find prey. Juveniles filter feed zooplankton from the water and adults feed on fish and squid.

74. Fiddler Stingray

Common name : Banjo shark, Fiddler, Green skate, Parrit, Southern fiddler ray
Scientific name : Trygonorrhina fasciata
Family : Rhinobatidae
Native to : Australia
Interesting fact : The egg capsule of the fiddler stingray is golden in colour.
Conservation status : Least Concern

Fiddler stingrays live in the shallow waters of sandy bays, rocky reefs and seagrass beds at depths of 120-180 metres. They are brown with geometric black or brown markings and venomous tail spines. They eat shellfish, crabs and worms at the bottom of the ocean by crushing with their jaws. These ovoviviparous creatures give birth to litters of 4-6.

75. Fiji Blue Devil Damsel Fish

Common name : Southseas devil, Southseas demoiselle, Fiji damsel
Scientific name : Chrysiptera taupou
Family : Pomacentridae
Native to : Western Pacific Ocean
Interesting fact : The male guards the eggs until they hatch.
Conservation status : Not Evaluated

This blue fish with neon-like reflections lives in lagoons and offshore coral reefs. It is an aggressive and territorial fish. It stays in the same colony for up to 2 years and can grow up to 8 cm in length. They pair up to breed. Feeding on zooplankton and phytoplankton they live up to 10 years.

76. Fin Whale

Common name : Fin-backed whale,
Finner, Common rorqual, Herring whale, Razorback
Scientific name : Balaenoptera physalus
Family : Balaenopteridae
Native to : Oceans worldwide
Interesting fact : Fin whales can swim up to a speed of 40 km per hour
Conservation status : Endangered

Measuring 18.5-22.0 metres long, fin whales are the second largest animals in the world. The brownish-grey whale has a prominent dorsal fin, a V-shaped rostrum and paired blowholes. They filter feed on small schooling fish, squid, crustaceans, copepods and krill. They mate in temperate waters during winter, followed by an eleven-month to a one-year gestation. Their lifespan is 94 years.

77. Firefly Squid

Common name : Japanese firefly squid,
Sparkling enope squid
Scientific name : Watasenia scintillans
Family : Enoploteuthidae
Native to : Western Pacific Ocean
Interesting fact : Every year, a natural lightshow happens in the coast of Japan as these squids gather for spawning.
Conservation status : Least Concern

The firefly squid is aptly named, as it emits a deep-blue light throughout its body due to the presence of photophores. They measure 3 inches at maturity and have eight arms and two tentacles. The light helps to attract prey, confuse predators and to communicate with potential mates. Its lifespan is one year.

78. Flamboyant Cuttlefish

Common name : Pfeffer's flamboyant cuttlefish
Scientific name : Metasepia pfefferi
Family : Sepiidae
Native to : Indo-Pacific Ocean
Interesting fact : Flamboyant cuttlefish is the only known poisonous cuttlefish.
Conservation status : Data Deficient

This colourful, flamboyant cuttlefish is patterned and can change its body colour in a flash. Measuring 8 cm, it has three pairs of papillae on the back, broad, blade-like arms and arm suckers arranged in four rows. With a small cuttlebone it can float only for a short time; instead, they walk on the sea floor and eat fish and crustaceans.

79. *Flamingo Tongue Snail*

Scientific name : Cyphoma gibbosum
Family : Ovulidae
Native to : Western Atlantic Ocean
Interesting fact : The mantle acts like gills absorbing oxygen and expelling carbon dioxide.
Conservation status : Not Evaluated

The flamingo tongue snail is a small, brightly coloured sea snail living on corals. The shell is covered by live, bright orange-yellow mantle tissue with black markings. When attacked, the mantle flaps retract exposing the shell. They are ectoparasites of corals and feed by scraping the polyps off the coral. Their lifespan is 2 years.

80. *Flounder (European)*

Common name : Baltic flounder, Mud flounder, River flounder, White fluke
Scientific name : Platichthys flesus
Family : Pleuronectidae
Native to : Oceans worldwide
Interesting fact : Flounders hide in the ocean floor with the eye-side facing up.
Conservation status : Least Concern

A flounder is a group of round, flatfish living in the ocean floor. It has both the eyes on any one side. Though there is one on each side of its brain while hatching, during metamorphosis one eye migrates resulting in the strange feature. They feed on spawns, crustaceans, polychaetes and small fish. Their lifespan is 12-14 years.

81. *Flower Hat Jelly*

Scientific name : Olindias formosus
Family : Olindiidae
Native to : Brazil, Argentina and Southern Japan
Interesting fact : The sting of a flower hat jelly can cause rashes in humans and blooms of these fish affect shrimp fishing.
Conservation status : Not Evaluated

A flower hat jelly looks like a colourful firework with its translucent bell and multi-coloured tentacles. Unlike other jellyfish, the rim of the bell too has tentacles that coil or uncoil as needed. This fish grows up to 15 cm in diameter with no head, heart, brain, cartilage or eyes. They catch small fish with their tentacles. Its lifespan is 4-6 months.

82. *Flying Fish*

Common name : Backspot flying fish
Scientific name : Cheilopogon dorsomacula
Family : Exocoetidae
Native to : Pacific Oceans
Interesting fact : Since a flying fish is attracted by light, a fisherman uses light to lure it to his boat.
Conservation status : Least Concern

The predators of the flying fish have a tough time catching them as they can glide out of water. Its long, wing-like pectoral fins help it leap out of water and propel itself into the air. At the end of the glide, it pushes itself for another glide. They can cover a distance of 655 feet this way. Feeding on plankton they live for 5 years.

83. *Four-eyed Butterfly Fish*

Common name : Butterbun, Kete, School mistress
Scientific name : Chaetodon capistratus
Family : Chaetodontidae
Native to : Western Atlantic Ocean
Interesting fact : This four-eyed butterfly fish makes an attractive aquarium fish due to its small size.
Conservation status : Least Concern

You may have seen this attractive fish in photos of coral reefs. It has a large false eye at the base of its tail to confuse its predators. It has a laterally compressed body, a single dorsal fin, a small mouth with tiny hair-like teeth to feed on coral polyps, tentacles of feather-dusters and Christmas-tree worms.

84. *Foxface*

Common name : Foxface rabbitfish
Scientific name : Siganus vulpinus
Family : Siganidae
Native to : Western Pacific Ocean
Interesting fact : When stressed or at night, it changes to a mottled brown-colour for better camouflage amongst rocks and sand.
Conservation status : Least Concern

The foxface lives in coral-rich areas feeding on macroalgae and zooplankton. It is bright yellow-coloured with black-and-white markings on the front of its body, growing to a size of up to 25 cm. It has a venomous spine on its dorsal, pectoral and anal fins which it stabs its predators with. Its lifespan is 8-12 years.

85. Frilled Shark

Common name : Lizard shark, Scaffold shark
Scientific name : Chlamydoselachus anguineus
Family : Chlamydoselachidae
Native to : Atlantic and Pacific Oceans
Interesting fact : This vivaparous shark has
a gestation period of three and a half years.
Conservation status : Near Threatened

Living near the bottom of outer continental shelf and upper continental slope at depths of up to 1,200 metres is the frilled shark. It is dark brown or grey, measures 2 metres long and has an eel-like body with six pairs of frilly gill slits. It bends its body and lunges forward like a snake to capture its prey, mainly cephalopods, bony fish and other sharks.

86. Ghost Pipefish

Common name : Ornate ghost pipefish, Harlequin ghost pipefish
Scientific name : Solenostomus paradoxus
Family : Solenostomidae
Native to : Indo-Pacific Ocean
Interesting fact : Inside the brooding pouch, branching stalks grow out of the skin and attach to the incubating eggs acting like an umbilical cord.
Conservation status : Not Evaluated

Ghost pipefish are experts at camouflage and the most beautiful. Measuring only 15 cm, they come in colours such as red, yellow, black or green with patterned spots. They float motionlessly sucking crustaceans and benthic shrimps with their long snouts. The females have enlarged and modified pelvic fins forming a brood pouch to incubate the eggs.

87. Giant Catfish

Common name : Mekong giant catfish
Scientific name : Pangasianodon gigas
Family : Pangasiidae
Native to : Mekong basin
Interesting fact : It is the largest freshwater fish in the world.
Conservation status : Critically Endangered

The giant catfish is a large fish that looks like a shark. It is grey to white in colour, lacking stripes, barbels and teeth. It grows rapidly to a length of 3 metres and a weight of 150-200 kg in six years. These cannibalistic fries feed on zooplankton, and become herbivores in a year feeding on filamentous algae. Their lifespan is 60 years.

88. *Giant Hatchetfish*

Common name : Greater silver hatchetfish
Scientific name : Argyropelecus gigas
Family : Sternoptychidae
Native to : Oceans worldwide except the North Pacific
Interesting fact : Giant hatchetfish can jump
out of water and catch mosquitoes and flies.
Conservation status : Not Evaluated

The giant hatchetfish lives deep in the sea with about 45 known species. Its extremely thin body resembles a hatchet. They have large, tubular eyes that point upwards enabling them to search for food above. Its entire body has photophores and can produce light. They migrate to shallower waters at night to feed on plankton and tiny fish. Their lifespan is less than a year.

89. *Giant Oar Fish*

Common name : King of herrings,
Ribbon fish, Oar fish
Scientific name : Regalecus glesne
Family : Regalecidae
Native to : Oceans worldwide except the poles
Interesting fact : The giant oar fish is the
world's longest bony fish growing up to 56 feet long.
Conservation status : Not Evaluated

The giant oar fish is silvery with dark markings, red fins, a ribbon-like body and long, oar-shaped pelvic fins. It is a solitary fish that swims with its dorsal fin, also swimming in vertical position. It feeds on krill, small crustaceans, small fish and squid. The eggs are 2.5 mm in size and float near the surface until hatching.

90. *Giant Squid*

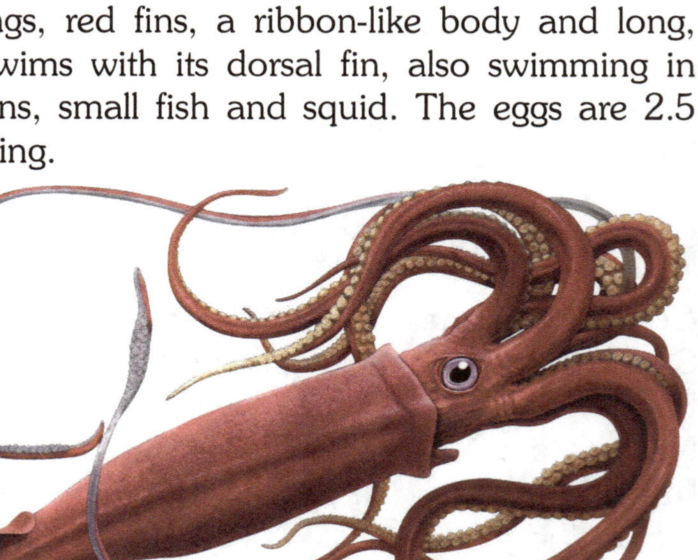

Scientific name : Architeuthis dux
Family : Architeuthidae
Native to : Oceans worldwide
Interesting fact : Giant squids have an
ammonium chloride solution running throughout
their bodies which helps maintain buoyancy.
Conservation status : Least Concern

The giant squid grows 10-13 metres long, possessing a mantle, eight arms and two longer tentacles. The arms and tentacles are lined with hundreds of suction cups, each mounted on a stalk, used to attach to its prey. It has a complex brain, a sophisticated nervous system and a closed circulatory system. These solitary hunters feed on fish and other squids.

91. Glass-eye Squirrel Fish

Common name : Balarton, Blotched bigeye, Dusky-finned bullseye, Moonshine conga, Rock bullseye
Scientific name : Heteropriacanthus cruentatus
Family : Priacanthidae
Native to : Oceans worldwide
Interesting fact : The glass-eye can make sounds to ward off intruders.
Conservation status : Not Evaluated

Living in coral reefs, lagoons, seaward reefs and rocky bottoms are these big-eyed fish. Juveniles have bodies covered with brown and red patches and become brighter with age. It has large eyes, a symmetrical body-shape, and small elliptical spots on the fins. Measuring 12 inches long, this nocturnal fish feeds on shrimp, squid, octopuses, crabs, small fish and polychaetes.

92. Great White Shark

Common name : White shark, White pointer
Scientific name : Carcharodon carcharias
Family : Lamnidae
Native to : Coastal waters worldwide
Interesting fact : The great white shark detects its prey by the electrical impulses from the body of the prey.
Conservation status : Vulnerable

Living as deep as 1,200 metres, the great white shark is the most dangerous shark in the world. It measures 4.0-5.2 metres long and weighs 680-1,100 kg. It has a conical snout and rows of serrated teeth behind the main ones. They are ovoviviparous with 11 month gestation period. Their lifespan is 70 years reaching sexual maturity at 30 years.

93. Grey Nurse Shark

Common name : Sand tiger shark, Spotted ragged-tooth shark
Scientific name : Carcharias taurus
Family : Odontaspididae
Native to : Sub-tropical and temperate waters worldwide
Interesting fact : They are the only known sharks that surface to gulp air and float.
Conservation status : Vulnerable

The grey nurse shark has a pointy head and a bulky grey body with reddish-brown spots. It has three rows of protruding, sharp teeth. It can grow up to 3 metres long. They hunt in groups for bony fishes, crustaceans, squid and other sharks. It exhibits intrauterine cannibalism, where the most developed embryo will feed upon its siblings.

94. Grouper (Tiger)

Common name : Tiger grouper
Scientific name : Mycteroperca tigris
Family : Epinephelidae
Native to : Western Atlantic Ocean
Interesting fact : Groupers are protogynous hermaphrodites, with a large male controlling harem of 15 females.
Conservation status : Least Concern

Groupers have stout bodies and large mouths with crushing tooth plates inside the pharynx. They can grow up to 1 metre long and weigh up to 100 kg. Its powerful gill muscles, together with the mouth, forms powerful sucking system pulling its prey in from a distance. It feeds on fish, octopuses and crustaceans. Its lifespan is 40 years.

95. Grunion

Common name : Gulf grunion
Scientific name : Leuresthes sardina
Family : Atherinopsidae
Native to : Pacific Ocean and Gulf of California
Interesting fact : Grunion runs are popular where people enjoy catching the spawning fish.
Conservation status : Near Threatened

Grunions are small, slender fish with blunt, rounded snouts. They have no teeth and feed on plankton. In an unusual mating ritual at high tide, females dig their tails into the sandy beaches to lay eggs and the eggs remain hidden for 10 days. At high tide, the eggs hatch and young ones are washed out to the sea.

96. Guadalupe Fur Seal

Scientific name : Arctocephalus townsendi
Family : Otariidae
Native to : Mexico's Guadalupe Island
Interesting fact : The mother makes alternate trips to sea returning to nurse the pup till it is 8-9 months old.
Conservation status : Least Concern

Living in volcanic caves along island shores is the guadalupe fur seal. It is dark brown with visible ear flaps and yellowish-tan coloured hair in the back of the neck. This fish takes a swim several times a day to cool off as it has thick fur. It feeds on rockfish and squid. Its lifespan is 17-20 years.

97. Haddock

Scientific name : Melanogrammus aeglefinus
Family : Gadidae
Native to : North Atlantic Ocean
Interesting fact : Haddock is
a popular food fish.
Conservation status : Vulnerable

Haddocks belong to the cod fish
family and live in cold waters that are
2-10 degrees. Juveniles stay in shallow
water while adults venture into the deeper sea. It has a black lateral line along its white side
and a distinctive spot above the pectoral fin called thumbprint or St. Peter's mark. It feeds
on small invertebrates; some adults feed on fish.

98. Hake

Common name : Cornish salmon,
European hake, Herring hake
Scientific name : Merluccius merluccius
Family : Merlucciidae
Native to : Atlantic Ocean and Pacific Ocean
Interesting fact : Hake is a popular food fish and can
be substituted in cod fish recipes.
Conservation status : Not Evaluated

About 12 species of hakes are known and they live close to the bottom at daytime and
move towards the surface at night. They are thin blue-grey fish and have black mouths with
sharp teeth. They grow 1 metre long and weigh 1-8 pounds. Adults feed on squid, whiting
and mackerel while juveniles feed on crustaceans. Their lifespan is 14 years.

99. Halibut

Common name : Atlantic halibut
Scientific name : Hippoglossus hippoglossus
Family : Pleuronectidae
Native to : North Pacific and North Atlantic Oceans
Interesting fact : The name halibut is derived from
'Hali' (holy) and 'butt' (flat fish), as it was eaten on
Catholic holidays.
Conservation status : Endangered

The halibut is a dark brown flat fish with an off-white belly and very small scales. One
of its eyes migrates to the other side at six months post-birth. It feeds on sand lances,
octopuses, crabs, salmons, hermit crabs, herring and flounder. It spends most of the time at
the bottom moving up the water column to feed. Its lifespan is 30-50 years.

100. Harlequin Tusk Fish

Scientific name : Choerodon fasciatus
Family : Labridae
Native to : Western Pacific Ocean
Interesting fact : It has large orbital eyes that move independently from each other.
Conservation status : Least Concern

Harlequin tusks live among reefs at depths of 5-35 metres. They are brightly coloured with shades of blue, green and orange. They have sharp protruding teeth that turn dark blue as they mature. These protogynous hermaphrodites are born as females and switch sex later in life. It feeds on echinoderms, crustaceans, molluscs and worms. Lifespan is 8 years.

101. Hawaiian Monk Seal

Scientific name : Neomonachus schauinslandi
Family : Phocidae
Native to : North-West Hawaiian Islands
Interesting fact : During mating males attack females, called mobbing, sometimes even killing them.
Conservation status : Endangered

Hawaiian monk seals prefer tropical waters unlike most seals that prefer cold waters. They are excellent swimmers adapted with large hind flippers and small front ones. They grow 7-8 feet long and weigh 300-600 pounds. They feed on bony fish, cephalopods and crustaceans. Females nurse pups for 6 weeks, never leaving the beach. Lifespan is 25-30 years.

102. Helmet Cowfish

Common name : Humpback turretfish, Camel cowfish, Thornbacked boxfish, Hovercraft boxfish
Scientific name : Tetrosomus gibbosus
Family : Ostraciidae
Native to : Indo-West Pacific Ocean
Interesting fact : The eyes of the helmet cowfish can move in different directions.
Conservation status : Least Concern

The helmet cowfish hovers around coral reefs, rocky areas, sand flats and grass beds. It grows up to 4 inches long. Two horns project from its head. It has large blue eyes and a tan body with patches of blue and black. A poisonous substance called ostracitoxin is released when it is stressed. It feeds on macroalgae, worms, crustaceans, molluscs and sponges.

103. Herring (Atlantic)

Common name : Atlantic herring, Bismark herring, Cleanplate herring, Golden cure
Scientific name : Clupea harengus
Family : Clupeidae
Native to : North Pacific and North Atlantic Oceans
Interesting fact : Herrings are a rich source of Omega-3 fatty acids and vitamin D for humans.
Conservation status : Least Concern

The herring is a group of 200 different species popular as food. It is silver-coloured with a single, soft dorsal fin and a protruding lower jaw. They can grow up to 46 cm long and weigh up to 700 gram. They live in large schools and feed on copepods, arrow worms, amphipods and krill. Their lifespan is 12-16 years.

104. Honeycomb Moray Eel

Common name : Laced moray, Tesselate moray, Honeycomb moray, Reticulated moray
Scientific name : Gymnothorax favagineus
Family : Muraenidae
Native to : Indo-Pacific Ocean
Interesting fact : Its skin secretes mucus protectin it from predators, parasites and infection and also helping it move faster in the water.
Conservation status : Not Evaluated

Living in crevices within reef flats and slopes are these honeycomb marked, snake-like fish. Their skins contain toxins produced by algae. They have dorsal fins running their entire length. With wide mouths that open and close, they might look threatening but it is only to let water in for respiration through gills. It feeds on small fish and invertebrates.

105. Horseshoe Crab

Scientific name : Limulus polyphemus
Family : Limulidae
Native to : Canada, Mexico and United States
Interesting fact : Their blood is blue due to hemocyanin and has amebocytes giving them immunity from pathogens.
Conservation status : Near Threatened

The horseshoe crab is found in sandy bottoms of oceans. It grows up to 60 cm long. A hard shell covers its entire body and has five pairs of legs that end with a claw, except the last pair. The crab has a long, rigid tail which is used to flip itself if it is turned over. It feeds on crustaceans and small fish.

106. Humpback Whale

Common name : Hump whale, Hunchbacked whale
Scientific name : Megaptera novaeangliae
Family : Balaenopteridae
Native to : Oceans worldwide
Interesting fact : Males sing a song for 10-20 minutes which they repeat for hours at a time.
Conservation status : Least Concern

The humpback whale is a species of baleen whale that feeds on small fish and krill with its bristle-like teeth. It grows up to 16 metres long and weighs up to 36,000 kg. The body is stocky with a hump and a fluked tail. They migrate to tropical waters to breed and give birth in winters. Their lifespan is 45-100 years.

107. Irukandji

Scientific name : Carukia barnesi
Family : Tamoyidae
Native to : Australia, British Isles, Japan and the Florida Coast of United States
Interesting fact : Due to its small size, it is hard to notice and can be fatal to humans.
Conservation status : Not Evaluated

The world's smallest jellyfish, irukandji is only 5-25 mm wide with four tentacles that are a metre long. This venomous jellyfish has stingers present in clumps around the bell and along the tentacles. It has a primitive, transparent eye on each side of the bell. It feeds on fish by stunning them with the venom.

108. Isopod

Scientific name : Porcellio pumicatus
Family : Porcellionidae
Native to : Worldwide Oceans
Interesting fact : The female broods its young ones in a pouch under the thorax.
Conservation status : Not Evaluated

Isopods are crustaceans living in land, sea and freshwater. They have segmented exoskeletons, two pairs of antennae, seven pairs of jointed limbs and five pairs of branching appendages on their abdomens for respiration. There are 10,000 species, most of them being marine. Their sizes range from 0.3 mm to 50 cm. They feed on mosses, bark, algae, fungi and decaying matter.

109. *John Dory*

Common name : Atlantic John dory, Doree, Gallocristo, Girti, St. Peter's fish
Scientific name : Zeus faber
Family : Zeidae
Native to : Coasts worldwide
Interesting fact : John dory's body is so thin that its hard to spot when viewed from the front.
Conservation status : Least Concern

The John dory lives near seabeds and has an olive-green body, a silvery belly and a large dark eye spot on the side which confuses prey. It feeds on fish like sardines, cuttlefish and squid. They mature at 3-4 years of age, spawning at the end of winter, releasing eggs and sperm in the water to fertilize. Their lifespan is 12 years.

110. *Juan Fernandez Fur Seal*

Scientific name : Arctocephalus philippii
Family : Otariidae
Native to : Juan Fernandez Islands
Interesting fact : The mother returning from the sea after feeding calls the pup on land with a characteristic call to nurse it.
Conservation status : Least Concern

Named after the island it is found in, the Juan Fernandez Fur Seal (like most seals) has an elongated body, a long and pointed snout and flippers. Their diet is made of squids, lobsters and fish. The female gives birth to a single pup and nurses it for 8-12 months. These fish were heavily hunted for their blubber, meat and oil between the 17th-19th centuries.

111. *Killer Whale*

Common name : Orca whale, Orca, Grampus
Scientific name : Orcinus orca
Family : Delphinidae
Native to : Oceans worldwide
Interesting fact : Killer whale uses echolocation for communication and locating its prey.
Conservation status : Data Deficient

The killer whale lives in family groups called pods, feeding on fish, seals, mammals, sea birds and sea turtles. It has a black back, white chest and sides, a large dorsal fin and strong teeth covered in enamel. They grow up to 5-8 metres long and weigh 3-6 tonnes. Their lifespan is 50 years for females and 29 years for males.

112. Lacy Scorpionfish

Common name : Merlet's scorpionfish, Weedy scorpionfish
Scientific name : Rhinopias aphanes
Family : Scorpaenidae
Native to : Western Pacific Ocean
Interesting fact : Lacy scorpionfish wait for the prey to come close and inhale it after lunging forward.
Conservation status : Not Evaluated

Aptly named, the lacy scorpionfish is lacy, with a large upturned mouth and tentacles on the snout. The spines on its back are venomous. These fish come in colours like yellow, brown, purple, green or black with a maze-like pattern, blending in with the background. It grows up to 30 cm long. This nocturnal creature feeds on fish and small invertebrates.

113. Lamprey

Common name : Sea lamprey
Scientific name : Petromyzon marinus
Family : Petromyzontidae
Native to : Worldwide Oceans
Interesting fact : Lampreys spawn in rivers and die shortly after.
Conservation status : Least Concern

About 38 species of these eel-like fish are found in coastal and freshwaters. It has a round, sucker-like, jawless mouth filled with rows of teeth, that act as parasites boring into the flesh of the other fish to suck blood. Some feed on small invertebrates. They grow 13-100 cm long. Young larvae spend several years in rivers, feeding on detritus and micro-organisms. Their lifespan is 7 years.

114. Largetooth Sawfish

Scientific name : Pristis pristis
Family : Pristidae

Native to : Indo-West Pacific Oceans
Interesting fact : A sawfish can replace its tooth if it is lost or worn out.
Conservation status : Critically Endangered

This sawfish looks quite menacing as it has a saw as its snout, with 14 to 22 very large teeth on each side. These are just scales and actual teeth are present inside its mouth. It grows up to 650 cm long and weighs 1200 pounds. It is ovoviviparous with 5 months gestation period. It feeds on fish and benthic invertebrates.

115. Lawnmower Blenny

Common name : Banded jewelled-blenny,
Banded blenny, Jewelled rockskipper
Scientific name : Salarias fasciatus
Family : Blenniidae
Native to : Australasia
Interesting fact : It has a hard jaw with which it delivers
a concussion-blow to fish and invertebrates confronting it.
Conservation status : Least Concern

The lawnmover blenny is found feeding on algae from dead corals. It has a pale, olive to brown body with white and blue spots and dark bands. They camouflage by turning darker when threatened. Males are territorial and dominant. It is oviparous with the eggs being demersal and adhesive. Its lifespan is 2-4 years.

116. Leaf Fish

Common name : South American leaf fish, Amazon leaf fish
Scientific name : Monocirrhus polyacanthus
Family : Polycentridae
Native to : Brazil, Peru, Venezuela,
Colombia, Bolivia
Interesting fact : Leaf fish are extremely agile hunters
catching fairly large prey and consuming it in a fraction of a second.
Conservation status : Not Evaluated

The leaf fish lives in brackish waters, mimicking a dead leaf, rarely moving and thus hiding from predators and prey. This 3-inch long fish has a large head and mouth. They feed on small fish, aquatic insects and invertebrates. Females lay eggs on or under the surface of leaves and males care for the fries. Their lifespan is 5-8 years.

117. Leafy Sea Dragon

Common name : Glauerts sea dragon
Scientific name : Phycodurus eques
Family : Syngnathidae
Native to : Australia
Interesting fact : Baby sea
dragons are independent from the
moment they hatch.
Conservation status : Near Threatened

Living around kelp-covered rocks and clumps in the sea is the beautifully camouflaged leafy sea dragon with its long leaf-like protrusion all over its body. A small, transparent pectoral fin on the ridge of the neck and a dorsal fin close to the tail are used for propulsion. Growing 20-24 cm long, they feed on crustaceans and plankton.

118. *Ling*

Common name : Common ling, European ling
Scientific name : Molva molva
Family : Lotidae
Native to : Atlantic Ocean
Interesting fact : The salted eggs of the ling are a popular delicacy in Spain.
Conservation status : Not Evaluated

The ling is a cod-like fish living in shallow coastal waters. Its slender body is 3 metres long. It has a small head, a small eye and a projecting upper jaw. The body is a marbled bronze-green with a dark spot at the hind edge of both dorsal fins. It feeds on all kinds of fish. Its Lifespan is 25 years.

119. *Lion Fish*

Common name : Hawaiian turkeyfish, Turkeyfish
Scientific name : Pterois sphex
Family : Scorpaenidae
Native to : Indo-Pacific Ocean
Interesting fact : The sting of a lion fish from its venomous dorsal fins can be quite painful to humans.
Conservation status : Not Evaluated

The lion fish is a venomous, hostile and territorial fish inhabiting reefs, corals, lagoons and rocky surfaces. It has red, white, creamy or black bands, showy pectoral fins, venomous spiky dorsal fins and a unique tentacle above the eye socket. It feeds on fish and shrimp. Females release two mucus-filled egg clusters containing about 15,000 eggs. Its lifespan is 5-10 years.

120. *Lion's Mane Jellyfish*

Common name : Lion's mane
Scientific name : Cyanea capillata
Family : Cyaneidae
Native to : Atlantic and Pacific Oceans
Interesting fact : Lion's mane jellyfish is the largest jellyfish in the world.
Conservation status : Not Evaluated

The lion's mane jellyfish gets its name from its tentacles. It has a pointed, star-like bell and tentacles of varying lengths; some are as long as 30 metres. It comes in colours like crimson, purple, orange and tan. Its diet is made of zooplankton, small fish, ctenophores and moon jellies. Capable of both sexual and asexual reproduction, it lives for a year.

121. *Live-bearing Seastar*

Scientific name : Parvulastra vivipara
Family : Asterinidae
Native to : South Australia
Interesting fact : They are hermaphrodites, fertilizing themselves and giving birth to live young, that emerge from an opening on the parents.
Conservation status : Vulnerable

Living in rocky crevices of calm, sheltered waterways are these tiny, orange seastars measuring only 13 mm in diameter. They are slow-moving and can easily be dislodged from rock surfaces. They live in colonies of 20 to 1,000; feeding on microscopic algae on the underside of submerged rocks. Their lifespan is 8-10 years.

122. *Lobster*

Common name : Red lobster
Scientific name : Eunephrops bairdii
Family : Nephropidae
Native to : Oceans worldwide
Interesting fact : They have blue blood due to the presence of hemocyanin.
Conservation status : Data Deficient

Lobsters are large marine crustaceans living in crevices and burrows on the sea floor. They have hard exoskeletons and 10 walking legs. The front 3 legs bear claws and the first leg is larger. They feed on fish, molluscs, crustaceans, worms and plants. They grow 25-50 cm in length. Their lifespan is 60 years.

123. *Longhorn Cowfish*

Common name : Trunkfish
Scientific name : Lactoria cornuta
Family : Ostraciidae
Native to : Indo-Pacific region
Interesting fact : It exudes a deadly toxin when stressed.
Conservation status : Not Evaluated

Aptly named, it has long horns on its head and inhabits coral reefs, lagoons, sandy and rocky bottoms. Its yellow-to-olive body has white or blue spots. It lacks gill cover and has hexagonal plate-like scales, fused into a triangular shell from which the fins and tail protrude. It feeds on benthic algae, sponges, worms, molluscs, crustaceans and small fish.

124. Mackerel (Blue)

Common name : Pacific mackerel, Japanese mackerel, Spotted mackerel
Scientific name : Scomber australasicus
Family : Scombridae
Native to : Atlantic and Pacific Oceans
Interesting fact : Eggs of mackerels float on water as they contain oily drops.
Conservation status : Least Concern

Mackerels are found in both temperate and tropical seas. They are torpedo-shaped, with vertical stripes, bluish-green backs, silvery bellies and deeply forked tails. Ranging in size from 14-16 inches long, they feed on plankton, crustaceans, molluscs, eggs of fish, shrimp, squid and small fish. Spawning is in spring and early summer along coastlines. Their lifespan is 15 years.

125. Mahi-Mahi

Common name : Common dolphin fish, Dolphin fish, Dorado, Green dolphin
Scientific name : Coryphaena hippurus
Family : Coryphaenidae
Native to : Oceans worldwide
Interesting fact : Mahi-mahi means strong-strong and these fish are fast swimmers with a speed of 57.5 km per hour.
Conservation status : Least Concern

This surface dwelling ray-finned fish is golden on the sides and bright blue and green on the back. The male has a protruding forehead whereas the female has a rounded head. It has a compressed body and a single dorsal fin extending from the head to the tail. They feed on flying fish, crabs, squid, mackerels and other forage fish. Their lifespan is 4-5 years.

126. Manatee (African)

Common name : Sea cow, West African manatee
Scientific name : Trichechus senegalensis
Family : Trichechidae
Native to : Florida
Interesting fact : It is the only animal that has a cornea connected to the blood stream.
Conservation status : Vulnerable

Manatees are large aquatic mammals that are up to 13 feet long and weigh up to 590 kg. A large upper lip is used to gather food and for communication. Their small eyes have eyelids that close in a circular manner. Surfacing for air regularly, these herbivores feed on freshwater and salt water plants. Its lifespan is 60 years.

127. *Mandarinfish*

Scientific name : Synchiropus splendidus
Family : Callionymidae
Native to : Australia and Indo-Pacific Oceans
Interesting fact : In the evenings, the mandarinfish surfaces to perform the dancing ritual for mating.
Conservation status : Not Evaluated

Mandarinfish are beautifully coloured fish living in reefs nd lagoons. They grow only up to 6 cm long and can be blue to yellow, orange, purple and green with wavy orange lines. They are highly reclusive during the day when they are seen among coral branches. They feed on small crustaceans, eggs of fish and other invertebrates. Their lifespan is 10-15 years.

128. *Manta Ray (Reef)*

Common name : Prince Alfred's ray, Inshore manta ray, Resident manta ray
Scientific name : Manta alfredi
Family : Mobulidae
Native to : Oceans worldwide
Interesting fact : The skin is covered in mucus protecting it from infections.
Conservation status : Vulnerable

Manta rays are large eagle rays that have triangular pectoral fins, horn-shaped cephalic fins and large mouths. They weigh up to 1,350 kg with broad heads and are black in colour with pale markings on their shoulders. They feed on zooplankton. Gestation period is 12-13 months producing one or two live pups. Lifespan is 50 years.

129. *Mimic Octopus*

Scientific name : Thaumoctopus mimicus
Family : Octopodidae
Native to : Indonesia and Malaysia
Interesting fact : The suckers have a touch sensor and chemoreceptor allowing the animal to taste its food.
Conservation status : Not Evaluated

The mimic octopus mimics the shape of other sea creatures to attract prey and avoid predators. It has 8 arms with 2 rows of suckers. Though its natural colour is light brown yet it sports white and brown stripes for a fierce look. It grows up to 60 cm long with tentacles about 25 inches long. Its lifespan is 9 months.

130. Moon Jelly

Common name : Common jelly, Saucer jelly
Scientific name : Aurelia aurita
Family : Ulmaridae
Native to : Atlantic, Pacific and Arctic Oceans
Interesting fact : The moon jellyfish lacks heart, brain, blood and gills.
Conservation status : Not Evaluated

The moon Jelly is translucent, 25-40 cm in diameter and has 4 horseshoe-shaped gonads, visible through the top of the bell. It respires by oxygen diffusion through the membrane covering its body. It drifts with the current feeding on plankton, molluscs, crustaceans and eggs of fish. They mate in spring and summer. Their lifespan is one year.

131. Moray Eel (Spotted)

Common name : White-chinned moray, Speckled moray, Common spotted moray
Scientific name : Gymnothorax moringa
Family : Muraenidae
Native to : Western Atlantic, North Carolina and Mexico
Interesting fact : An extra set of jaw and teeth in its throat allows it to break up food and digest it.
Conservation status : Least Concern

About 200 species of moray eels are known. These fish live in holes and crevices of rocks and corals. They can be black, brown, grey or olive green with long bodies and snouts. These snake-like fish lack pectoral and pelvic fins. Being dimly sighted, they use their excellent sense of smell to ambush prey like small fish, molluscs, cephalopods, sea snakes and crustaceans.

132. Mulberry Oyster Borer

Common name : Purpura marginalba
Scientific name : Tenguella marginalba
Family : Muricidae
Native to : Australia and Indo-Pacific region
Conservation status : Not Evaluated

The mulberry oyster borer is a sea snail that has a strong, conical shell with 5 rows of purple or blackish, square nodules giving it a mulberry appearance. True to its name, it drills holes in its victim's shell with its rough tongue and the sulphuric acid in its saliva dissolves the shell. It feeds on oysters, tubeworms, molluscs and barnacles.

133. Mulloway

Common name : Jewfish, Dusky kob, Butterfish, Japanese meagre, River kingfish, School jew, Silver jewfish, Southern meagre
Scientific name : Argyrosomus japonicas
Family : Sciaenidae
Native to : Indo-Pacific region
Interesting fact : Mulloways have large ear bones which are collected for jewellery.
Conservation status : Endangered

The mulloway is a silver to bronze-green fish growing to a length of 2 metres and weighing 30 kg. It has shield-like scales, a concave tail and a row of spots along the lateral line. Spawning is in marine waters just outside the surf zone. It feeds on fish, molluscs and crustaceans. Its lifespan is 30 years.

134. Mussel (Blue)

Common name : Blue mussel, Common mussel
Scientific name : Mytilus edulis
Family : Mytilidae
Native to : Temperate seas worldwide
Interesting fact : Freshwater mussels are used for pearl cultivation.
Conservation status : Endangered

Mussels are bivalve molluscs that have wide, asymmetrical shells that are dark blue, black or brown with a silvery nacreous interior. The shell has a tongue shaped organ called a foot, which has strong and elastic byssal threads for attaching to a firm substrate and for defence. They are filter-feeders, feeding on plankton and other microscopic sea creatures. Their lifespan is 4-24 years.

135. Narwhal

Common name : Unicorn whale
Scientific name : Monodon monoceros
Family : Monodontidae
Native to : Arctic Ocean

Interesting fact : Narwhals communicate with clicks, whistles and knocks.
Conservation status : Near Threatened

Narwhals are toothed whales that feed on flatfish, Arctic doe and polar cod. The male has a tusk-like, protruding upper canine tooth. They are dark when born and become whiter with age, mottled in brown markings. They are 3.95 to 5.50 metres long and weigh 800-1,600 kg. They mate and give birth to one calf in 14 months. Their lifespan is 50 years.

136. Needlefish (Atlantic)

Common name : Northern needlefish, Garfish, Swordfish
Scientific name : Strongylura marina
Family : Belonidae
Native to : Atlantic Oceans
Interesting fact : Needlefish can jump out of water at a speed of 38 metres per hour.
Conservation status : Least Concern

The needlefish has an elongated jaw and a slender body. It is silvery with a blue-green back having a single dorsal fin and a long narrow beak. The upper jaw grows fully only in adulthood. Juveniles have half beaks and feed on plankton. Adults feed on small fish, krill, crustaceans and small cephalopods. They reproduce through mating and laying eggs.

137. Nemertea

Common name : Nightingale ribbon worm
Scientific name : Katechonemertes nightingaleensis
Family : Prosorhochmidae
Native to : Worldwide Oceans
Interesting fact : Nemertea can shrink to one-tenth of its size.
Conservation status : Vulnerable

Nemerteas are very slim worms and less than 20 cm long with patterns of yellow, orange, red and green colouration. They have proboscis emerging just above their mouths, which turn inside-out to capture prey. They move very slowly using external cilia to glide. They feed on annelids, clams and crustaceans. Eggs are fertilized externally. Their lifespan is one year.

138. Northern Snakehead

Common name : Amur snakehead
Scientific name : Channa argus
Family : Channidae
Native to : Russia, China, North Korea and South Korea
Interesting fact : It has specialized organs for aquatic and aerial respiration, allowing it to live outside water for several days.
Conservation status : Not Evaluated

The Northern snakehead is a freshwater fish that is golden to pale brown with dark spots. It has a small, anteriorly depressed head and a large mouth with villiform teeth and large canines on the lower jaw. It feeds on crustaceans, other invertebrates and amphibians. Females discharge eggs over the nest, which are externally fertilized by males.

139. Nudibranch

Common name : Spanish shawl nudibranch
Scientific name : Flabellina iodinea
Family : Flabellinidae
Native to : Oceans worldwide
Interesting fact : They are hermaphrodites, having reproductive organs for both sexes, but cannot fertilize themselves.
Conservation status : Not Evaluated

    The nudibranch is an extraordinarily coloured mollusc. They are soft-bodied, shedding their shells after the larval stage. Measuring 20-600 mm long, they have tentacles which are sensitive to touch, taste and smell. Eggs get deposited within a gelatinous spiral. They feed on sponges, hydroids, bryozoans, sea slugs, tunicates, barnacles and anemones. Lifespan is less than one year.

140. Orange-spotted Filefish

Common name : Harlequin filefish, Beaked leatherjacket, Longnose filefish
Scientific name : Oxymonacanthus longirostris
Family : Monacanthidae
Native to : Indo-Pacific Ocean
Interesting fact : It rests in between branches of acropora corals looking like a piece of the reef.
Conservation status : Not Evaluated

    The orange spotted filefish is found in lagoons and coral reefs feeding exclusively on acropora polyps. It is found in pairs or in small groups on clumps of algae. It is pale blue with eight rows of orange-yellow patches, a long snout and a small upturned mouth. It is monogamous, spawning between May and October, eggs hatching just after sunset on the second day. Lifespan is 4-5 years.

141. Ostracod

Common name : Seed shrimp
Scientific name : Zonocypretta kalimna
Family : Cypridinidae
Native to : Oceans worldwide
Interesting fact : The eggs of the ostracods can survive complete drying and still be viable after many years.
Conservation status : Vulnerable

    Living really deep at 7000 metres are these small crustaceans, around 0.2-30.0 mm in size. They have flattened bodies with bivalve-like calcareous shells. Two pairs of antennae on the head help it swim. It lacks gills, heart and a circulatory system. They take in oxygen through bronchial plates on the body-surface. They feed on diatoms, bacteria, detritus and algae.

142. Oyster (Pacific)

Common name : Japanese oyster, Portuguese oyster
Scientific name : Crassostrea gigas
Family : Ostreidae
Native to : Oceans worldwide
Interesting fact : Oysters can filter up to 10 litres of water in an hour for feeding.
Conservation status : Least Concern

Oysters are immobile molluscs found clinging to shipwrecks, debris and harbour walls. They are divided into four groups: true oysters that are consumed by humans, pearl oysters that produce pearls, thorny oysters and saddle oysters having very thin shells. They open to breathe and feed on plankton. Eggs are released into the water where they are fertilized. Lifespan is 1-3 years.

143. Pacific Krill

Common name : North Pacific krill
Scientific name : Euphausia pacifica
Family : Euphausiidae
Native to : Northern Pacific Ocean
Interesting fact : Pacific krills migrate vertically in the night and act as food for surface predators.
Conservation status : Not Evaluated

Pacific krill are small crustaceans that are important food of baleen whales. They are 16-25 mm long, showing bioluminescent qualities. They have visible external gills, large black eyes and large abdomens. They filter-feed on phytoplankton, occasionally feeding on zooplankton. Females can release 20,000 eggs at a time in small clusters. Their lifespan is 6-10 years.

144. Pacific Sea Nettle

Common name : West coast sea nettle
Scientific name : Chrysaora fuscescens
Family : Pelagiidae
Native to : East Pacific Ocean
Interesting fact : The jellyfish has light detecting organs to help it migrate to the surface from the dark and deep waters.
Conservation status : Not Evaluated

The Pacific sea nettle is a jellyfish with a transparent to golden-brown bell. They have long, spiralling, white oral arms and 24 maroon tentacles. They catch their prey by their tentacles before stinging and paralysing it. They feed on zooplankton, crustaceans, pelagic snails, small fish, eggs of fish, larvae and jellyfish. They are capable of both sexual and asexual reproduction.

145. Pacific Torpedo Ray

Common name : Pacific torpedo, Pacific electric ray
Scientific name : Torpedo californica
Family : Torpedinidae
Native to : North-Eastern Pacific Ocean
Interesting fact : They can generate up to 45 volts of electricity in defence.
Conservation status : Least Concern

The Pacific torpedo ray is a fish that is slate grey or brown with dark spots and a white belly. It grows up to 1.4 metres long and weighs 41 kg. They have paired respiratory openings behind the eyes, rounded pectoral fins and thick tails with two dorsal fins. This solitary and nocturnal creature feeds on bony fish, cephalopods and invertebrates.

146. Pajama Cardinalfish

Common name : Polka-dot cardinalfish, Spotted cardinalfish, Coral cardinalfish, Red spotted cardinalfish
Scientific name : Sphaeramia nemanoptera
Family : Apogonidae
Native to : Western Pacific Oceans
Interesting fact : The mucus secreted from its skin protects it from parasites and infections.

The pajama cardinalfish inhabits very shallow waters around large stands of staghorn corals. This 3-inch long fish has a yellow head, a blue jaw, bright red eyes, a black midsection with a checkered board pattern and a spotted rear. They feed on zooplankton, eggs of fish, polychaete worms and small fish. They spawn every 3 or 4 weeks with males being mouthbrooders.

147. Pantropical-spotted Dolphin

Common name : Bridled dolphin, Narrow-snouted dolphin
Scientific name : Stenella attenuata
Family : Delphinidae
Native to : Temperate and tropical oceans worldwide
Interesting fact : They use echolocation, high-pitched clicks, that bounce back, to locate their prey.
Conservation status : Least Concern

This pantropical-spotted dolphin is one of the smallest dolphins with white speckles on a dark back. They have beak-like pointed snouts and sickle-shaped dorsal fins. Living in groups called pods, they grow 8 feet long and weigh 200-255 kg. They are good swimmers and perform acrobatic feats. It gives birth to a calf, after 11 months of gestation.

148. Peacock Mantis Shrimp

Common name : Harlequin mantis shrimp, Painted mantis shrimp, Clown mantis shrimp
Scientific name : Odontodactylus scyllarus
Family : Odontodactylidae
Native to : Indo-Pacific Oceans
Interesting fact : They have a complex vision and are able to see ultraviolet, polarized and regular light.
Conservation status : Not Evaluated

With beautiful peacock colours, this shrimp is found burrowing U-shaped holes near coral reefs. It can grow 3-18 cm long. The male has a green and blue exoskeleton while the female has a red one. This extremely territorial crustacean uses its club-shaped raptorial appendages to smash its prey like gastropods, crustaceans and bivalves. Reproduction is by internal fertilization. Its lifespan is 15-20 years.

149. Pharaoh Cuttlefish

Scientific name : Sepia pharaonis
Family : Sepiidae
Native to : Indian to the Pacific Ocean
Interesting fact : They shoot a cloud of black ink at predators when threatened.
Conservation status : Data Deficient

Living on coral and rocky reefs are the pharoah cuttlefish. With flat bodies, they are camouflaged easily while hovering near the ocean floor. Their mantles grow 42 cm long and they weigh up to 5 kg. They feed on small fish, crustaceans and other cuttlefish. They gather in thousands to spawn and live for 240 days.

150. Picasso Trigger

Common name : White-banded triggerfish
Scientific name : Rhinecanthus aculeatus
Family : Balistidae
Native to : Indo-Pacific region
Interesting fact : Spawning occurs around sunrise with eggs hatching around sunset.
Conservation status : Not Evaluated

The picasso trigger is a colourful fish found on reefs and sand flats. It is white with dark bands extending from its anal fin and a dark band over the eyes with blue lines. Sponges, stony corals, molluscs, crustaceans, worms, brittle stars and sea urchins make up their diet. It is territorial, guarding the eggs fiercely. Its lifespan is 10-15 years.

151. Pilchard (European)

Common name : Sardine, Soused pilchards, True sardine, Fair maid
Scientific name : Sardina pilchardus
Family : Clupeidae
Native to : North-East Atlantic, Iceland, North sea, Senegal, Mediterranean, Sea of marmara Black sea
Conservation status : Least Concern

Pilchards are migratory fish migrating northward in summer and southward in winter. They live in large schools near the water surface. They grow in length from 15-30 cm and have flat elongated bodies covered with large silvery scales. They rise to the surface at night and filter-feed on plankton.

152. Pinecone Fish

Common name : Pineapple fish, Knight fish
Scientific name : Cleidopus gloriamaris
Family : Monocentridae
Native to : Indian and Pacific Oceans
Interesting fact : It has bioluminescent organs (under the lower jaw) that are used to communicate and attract prey.
Conservation status : Not Evaluated

The pinecone fish are yellowish-orange in colour having rounded bodies covered completely with plate-like scales and large eyes. They live in large schools in ledges, caves, rocky flats and coral reefs at depths of 30 to 250 metres. They are nocturnal, resting in caves and crevices during the day and coming out at night to feed on zooplankton.

153. Pink Skunk Clownfish

Common name : Pink anemonefish, Salmon clownfish
Scientific name : Amphiprion perideraion
Family : Pomacentridae
Native to : Asia-Pacific region
Interesting fact : It is a protandeous hermaphrodite– the largest male in a group of about 8 fishes becomes a female.
Conservation status : Not Evaluated

The pink skunk clownfish lives among sea anemones in reef lagoons and outer reef slopes. It grows to a length of 4-7 cm. It has a peach-orange colour with one white stripe behind the head running the entire length of the back and another white stripe behind the eyes. It feeds on macro algae, diatoms, tunicates, copepods and benthic worms.

154. *Pinniped*

Common name : Guadalupe fur seal
Scientific name : Arctocephalus townsendi
Family : Diodontidae
Native to : North Atlantic, North Pacific and Southern Oceans
Interesting fact : The eyesight and hearing of pinnipeds are adapted for both air and water.
Conservation status : Least Concern

Pinnipeds are semi-aquatic marine mammals found in polar and sub-polar regions. They are comprised of walruses, sea lions, fur seals and the earless or true seals. They are 1-5 metres long and weigh 45-3200 kg. They have streamlined bodies and four flippers. They feed on fish, marine invertebrates and sea birds. Its lifespan is 25-30 years.

155. *Piranha*

Common name : Wimple piranha
Scientific name : Catoprion mento
Family : Serrasalmidae
Native to : South America
Interesting fact : The thin lateral line running from the head to tail is a sense organ that detects pressure changes in water and helps navigate through obstacles.
Conservation status : Not Evaluated

Piranhas have sharp, interlocking teeth and powerful jaws. They have a voracious appetite for meat, using their teeth for rapid puncture and shearing. Their large eyes are adapted for close-up vision. They feed on insects, fish, crustaceans, worms and other plant materials. They dig pits to lays eggs during breeding and swim around to protect them. Lifespan is 20-25 years.

156. *Plankton*

Native to : Waters worldwide
Conservation status : Not Evaluated

Plankton are organisms living in oceans, seas or freshwater bodies throughout the world.These include drifting animals, protists, archaea, algae and bacteria. They are divided into phytoplankton (producers capable of photosynthesis), zooplankton (feeding on other plankton) and bacterioplankton (recyclers such as bacteria or archaea). They cannot swim against the current and act as food to many large aquatic animals.

157. Porcupine Fish

Common name : Blowfish, Balloonfish, Globefish
Scientific name : Diodon holocanthus
Family : Diodontidae
Native to : Tropical and temperate waters worldwide
Interesting fact : Porcupine fish can inflate its body by swallowing air or water.
Conservation status : Not Evaluated

Similar to the pufferfish, the porcupine fish has spines on its back that are raised when it inflates its body to almost twice its size for defence. They live in coral, rocky reefs, mangroves, muddy, sandy and grassy flats. They can grow up to 36 inches long and are nocturnal feeding on snails, hermit crabs and sea urchins.

158. Porpoise

Common name : Mereswine
Scientific name : Phocoenidae
Family : Phocoenidae
Native to : Oceans worldwide
Interesting fact : Porpoises use echolocation to locate their prey.
Conservation status : Critically Endangered

Porpoises are dolphin-like, but much smaller aquatic mammals. Also related to whales, they have small, round heads and blunt jaws lined with spade-shaped teeth. They can grow up to 2.5 metres long and weigh 130-200 kg. They can dive up to 200 metres and feed on fish, squid and crustaceans. Gestation period is 11 months. Lifespan is 8-10 years.

159. Portuguese Man o' War

Common name : Bluebottle, Jellyfish, Stinging bluebottle, Stinger
Scientific name : Physalia physalis
Family : Physaliidae
Native to : Pacific, Indian and Atlantic Oceans
Interesting fact : The tentacles have nematocysts that are extremely venomous and deliver painful stings, killing prey.
Conservation status : Not Evaluated

Though the Portuguese man o' war looks like a jellyfish yet it is actually a colony of organisms called zooids. It has translucent tentacles at one end that are tinged blue, purple, pink or mauve. These can be 10-50 metres long and are used continuously for fishing in the water for small fish and shrimps. Their lifespan is one year.

160. *Prawn*

Common name : Giant tiger prawn
Scientific name : Penaeus monodon
Family : Penaeidae
Native to : Oceans and worldwide seas
Interesting fact : While molting, a prawn reabsorbs most of the protein and chitin from the old shell, as the new shell forms underneath.
Conservation status : Least Concern

Prawns belong to the sub-order Dendrobranchiata, and are found in the warmer waters of the tropical regions. They are crustaceans with shells, five pairs of swimming legs, five pairs of walking legs, three with claws and tails. They have branched-out gills and periodically molt, shedding their shells to grow. They feed on fish, krill, copepods, phytoplankton and detritus. Lifespan is 4-5 years.

161. *Pufferfish*

Common name : Guineafowl puffer, White-spotted puffer
Scientific name : Arothron meleagris
Family : Tetraodontidae
Native to : Indian and Pacific Oceans
Interesting fact : Sharks are the only species that can eat pufferfish without any side-effects to their toxin.
Conservation status : Least Concern

Pufferfish can quickly ingest water and enlarge into a balloon for defence. More than 120 species are known. They have thick, rough skins with small spines that stand out when they inflate. Their teeth are fused into plates for crushing the shells of crustaceans, snails, sea urchins and molluscs. They contain lethal doses of tetrodotoxin that can kill humans.

162. *Quahog*

Common name : Hard clam, Round clam
Scientific name : Mercenaria mercenaria
Family : Veneridae
Native to : North America, Central America, New England and Canada
Interesting fact : Quahogs begin their life as males and change their sex in successive years.
Conservation status : Not Evaluated

Quahogs are marine bivalve burrowing molluscs. They grow 1-4 inches wide and their shells are white or grey with dark rings. It has a muscular foot for moving through the mud. Spawning is in late spring to early summer. They filter water through their shells absorbing phytoplankton, bacteria and oxygen. Lifespan is 30 years.

163. Queen Conch

Common name : Giant conch, Pink conch
Scientific name : Lobatus gigas
Family : Strombidae
Native to : North-Western Atlantic
Interesting fact : The queen conch lays its eggs in long gelatinous strings on sand or seagrass.
Conservation status : Critically Endangered

The queen conch is a sea snail living in seagrass beds. It has a spiral shell with spines that has a pink, flared lip. It has large stalked eyes and a pair of sensory tentacles, a strong foot and a sickle-shaped operculum. They feed on macroalgae, seagrass, unicellular algae and detritus. Lifespan is 20-30 years.

164. Queensland Blenny

Scientific name : Ecsenius mandibularis
Family : Blenniidae
Native to : Western Pacific Ocean
Interesting fact : The body of the queensland blenny is protected by a layer of slime.
Conservation status : Not Evaluated

Found living in coral reefs is the queensland blenny, a fish that is 7.5 cm long and has an elongated, tapering body with a long dorsal fin. It is herbivorous, feeding on plants, benthic algae and weeds. This territorial fish enjoys digging and jumping. They are oviparous with males attending the eggs until they hatch.

165. Queensland Giant Grouper

Common name : Brindlebass, Brown spotted cod
Scientific name : Epinephelus lanceolatus
Family : Serranidae
Native to : Indo-Pacific region except the Persian Gulf
Interesting fact : Living up to 50 years, the colour of the fish dulls with age.
Conservation status : Vulnerable

One of the world's largest bonyfish, the queensland giant grouper lives in coral reefs. They can be 3 metres long and weigh up to 600 kg. Adults are green-grey to grey-brown with faint mottling. Its mouth is lined with seven rows of teeth on the middle of its lower jaw. It feeds on small sharks, sea turtles, lobsters, crustaceans and bonyfish.

166. Quillfish

Scientific name : Ptilichthys goodie
Family : Ptilichthyidae
Native to : North Pacific Ocean
Interesting Fact : They can be found on the surface at night attracted by the light of fishing boats.
Conservation status : Not Evaluated

The quillfish is a slender, elongated, eel-like fish growing up to 34 cm long. It has over 230 vertebrae and many rayed fins. It burrows in sandy and muddy bottoms during the day, emerging at dusk to feed. It makes significant seasonal migrations of less than 200 km at particular times of the year for breeding or hibernation.

167. Red Face Hermit Crab

Common name : White-spotted hermit crab, Spotted hermit crab
Scientific name : Dardanus megistos
Family : Diogenidae
Native to : Oceans worldwide
Interesting fact : As the crab grows in size, it looks for a larger shell and abandons the old one.
Conservation status : Not Evaluated

The red face hermit crab is not a true crab and is found living in estuaries, intertidal areas and reefs. It has 5 pairs of legs and a long, soft, spirally curved abdomen protected by salvaged empty shells of molluscs. They feed on mussels, small plankton, worms, dead plants and animals. Eggs are carried and hatched in a mass.

168. Red Indianfish

Common name : Australian prowfish, Red foreheadfish
Scientific name : Pataecus fronto
Family : Pataecidae
Native to : Australia
Interesting fact : The red Indianfish sheds its skin periodically to get rid of parasites.
Conservation status : Not Evaluated

True to its name, the red Indianfish is brown to reddish-orange in colour with dark blotches. It has a compressed body and a long dorsal fin, stretching its entire length. It lacks pelvic fins and scales. It grows up to 35 cm long and weighs 0.851 kg. This slow-moving, territorial fish feeds on shrimps and other crustaceans. Its lifespan is 45 years.

169. *Red-lipped Batfish*

Common name : Galapagos batfish, Rosy-lipped batfish
Scientific name : Ogcocephalus darwini
Family : Ogcocephalidae
Native to : South-East Pacific Oceans
Interesting fact : The lure on its head secretes a chemical that attracts the prey.
Conservation status : Least Concern

The red-lipped batfish really looks like it's wearing lipstick and rests partially covered in sand. It is creamy-beige to emerald green and its dorsal fin becomes a single spine-like projection on its head to lure prey. It has modified pectoral, pelvic and anal fins to rest and walk on the sea floor. It feeds on small fish and crustaceans.

170. *Red Sea Urchin*

Scientific name : Strongylocentrotus franciscanus
Family : Strongylocentrotidae
Native to : Pacific Ocean
Interesting fact : The red sea urchin has no visible legs, eyes, heart or brain.
Conservation status : Near Threatened

The red sea urchin is a spine-covered creature with a spherical body enclosed in a hard shell. Found living in rocky shores, they crawl slowly on the sea floor with their spines and the tube feet scattered amidst them. With its mouth located on its underside surrounded by five teeth, it feeds on seaweeds, kelp and algae. Its lifespan is 30 years.

171. *Red Waratah Anemone*

Common name : Red beadlet anemone, Cherry anemone, Kotore anemone
Scientific name : Actinia tenebrosa
Family : Actiniidae
Native to : Eastern Australia and New Zealand
Interesting fact : The anemone is viviparous, brooding its young ones inside the column, releasing them through the mouth when they are fully developed.
Conservation status : Not Evaluated

This small, brown-red anemone lives in intertidal rocky shores. It is a large polyp with feeding tentacles held up on a cylindrical body or 'column'. The basal disc keeps it fixed to a substrate and helps it move. The tentacles have hundreds of stinging cells called nematocysts to catch prey like plankton and small fish. Its lifespan is 80 years.

172. *Reef Stonefish*

Common name : Fish stone, Reef stone, Poison scorpionfish, Dornorn
Scientific name : Synanceia verrucosa
Family : Synanceiidae
Native to : Indo-Pacific Ocean and Northern Australia
Interesting fact : The reef stonefish is highly venomous, with spines in its dorsal fin that inject venom into its prey and even humans.
Conservation status : Critically Endangered

    The reef stonefish is brilliantly camouflaged. Lying like a stone or a coral in coral reef, rocky, muddy and sandy bottoms, this fish is brown or grey with areas of yellow, orange or red. It can grow 30-40 cm long and weigh nearly 5 pounds. It feeds on fish, shrimp and other crustaceans. Lifespan is 5-10 years.

173. *Requiem Shark*

Common name : Sawtooth shark
Family : Carcharhinidae
Native to : Temperate and tropical oceans worldwide
Interesting fact : Requiem sharks are the second largest group of sharks and are highly dangerous to humans.
Conservation status : Near Threatened

    Requiem sharks are migratory sharks found in warm coastal waters and coral reefs. They are 3-18 feet long, grey or brown with round eyes, have blade-like teeth with single cusps and five gill slits. These strong swimmers feed on sharks, rays, squid, octopuses, lobsters, turtles, mammals and sea birds. The young ones are born fully developed. Lifespan is 8-20 years.

174. *Ribbon Eel*

Common name : Ribbon moray, Black ribbon eel, Blue ribbon eel, Yellow ribbon eel
Scientific name : Rhinomuraena quaesita
Family : Muraenidae
Native to : Indo-Pacific Ocean
Interesting fact : They are sequential hermaphrodites, developing female parts as they grow, until they are able to lay eggs.
Conservation status : Least Concern

    Ribbon eels are found in lagoons or coastal reefs. Their long, thin bodies have broad dorsal and anal fins giving them a ribbon-like appearance. Their leaf-like nostril flaps sense vibrations in the water. Adult males are blue with yellow dorsal fins while yellow females have black anal fins. They feed on small fish and other marine creatures.

175. *Rose Fish*

Common name : Atlantic redfish, Norway haddock,
Red perch, Red bream, Golden redfish, Hemdurgan
Scientific Name : Sebastes marinus
Family : Sebastidae
Native to : North Atlantic Ocean
Interesting fact : The young ones of the
rose fish are brown in colour.
Conservation status : Not Evaluated

The rose fish is bright red, flattened sideways with a large bony head, large eyes, large mouth and jaws with many teeth. They grow up to 1 metres long and are viviparous, attaining sexual maturity at 9-10 inches of length. They feed on small fish, invertebrates and crustaceans. There lifespan is 60 years.

176. *Salmon (Atlantic)*

Common name : Atlantic Salmon
Scientific Name : Salmo salar
Family : Salmonidae
Native to : North Atlantic and
Pacific Oceans
Interesting fact : The age of a
salmon can be determined by the rings on the otolith, its earbone.
Conservation status : Least Concern

Salmons, being anadromous, are born in freshwater, migrate to the ocean and then return to the birth spot to spawn. Due to periods of rapid growth in summer followed by a period of slower growth in winter, rings form around its earbone, called the otolith. They feed on terrestrial and aquatic insects, amphipods, crustaceans and fish. Lifespan is 3-8 years.

177. *Scalloped Hammerhead Shark*

Scientific name : Sphyrna lewini
Family : Sphyrnidae
Native to : Atlantic, Indian and Pacific Oceans
Interesting fact : The hammer of the shark is
made of cartilage and has sensory organs that detect
changes in the water.
Conservation status : Endangered

The shark has a hammer on its head with the eyes and nostrils on its extended tips. It has a slim, brown-grey to bronze body with a white belly. They grow 370-430 cm long and weigh up to 152 kg. They feed on fish, squids and octopuses. They give birth to 15-30 live young ones after 9-10 months of gestation. Their lifespan is 30 years.

178. *Sea Cucumber (Leopard)*

Common name : Leopard sea cucumber
Scientific name : Bohadschia argus
Family : Holothuriidae
Native to : Indian and Pacific Oceans
Interesting fact : Sea cucumbers
communicate by sending hormone signals
through the water.
Conservation status : Least Concern

    Shaped like a cucumber, the sea cucumber lives on the sea floor. They have leathery skins and are 10-30 cm long. The endoskeleton below the skin is joined by connective tissues enabling it to squeeze through the smallest of gaps. They discharge a toxic chemical that kills animals in the vicinity. They feed on detritus and help recycle nutrients.

179. *Sea Goblin*

Common name : Demon stinger, Devil stinger
Scientific name : Inimicus didactylus
Family : Synanceiidae
Native to : Western Indo-Pacific Ocean
Conservation status : Not Evaluated

    Masters of camouflage, sea goblins are venomous fish with spines on their backs. Found buried in sandy areas or on coral outcrops, they wait for their prey and catch it by surprise. They are nocturnal, feeding on fish and invertebrates. They move by crawling very slowly along the seabed, using the four lower rays of their pectoral fins as legs.

180. *Seahorse*

Common name : Short snouted seahorse
Scientific name : Hippocampus hippocampus
Family : Syngnathidae
Native to : Oceans worldwide
Interesting fact : The male has a pouch on the ventral side, used for carrying the eggs.
Conservation status : Data Deficient

    The seahorse has a horse-like head and lives in seagrass beds, estuaries and coral reefs. They grow 1.5-35.5 cm long and swim upright. Bony but scale-less, they have flexible necks, long snouts and eyes that move independent of each other. They rest with their prehensile tails wound around stationary objects. They feed on small crustaceans, invertebrates and larval fish.

181. Sea Pens (Common)

Common name : Common sea pens, Phosphorescent sea pens
Scientific name : Pennatula phosphorea
Family : Pennatulidae
Native to : Worldwide Oceans
Interesting fact : Each sea pen is a colony of either male or emale polyps that release sperms and eggs in the water column for fertilization.
Conservation status : Endangered

Sea pens are brightly coloured, colony of polyps, that look like a quilled pen. A single polyp develops into a rigid, erect stalk, losing its tentacles and forming a peduncle at its base that is buried into the sand. They feed on plankton with their feather-like tentacles. They show bioluminescence and also provide shelter for other animals. Lifespan is 14-15 years.

182. Shovel-headed Mullet

Common name : Sharpnose mullet, Brown mullet
Scientific name : Neomyxus leuciscus
Family : Mugilidae
Native to : Pacific Ocean
Interesting fact : Eating this fish is claimed to cause hallucination.
Conservation status : Not Evaluated

The shovel-headed mullet lives in sandy shores, tide pools and rocky areas. They grow up to 46 cm long and live in large schools. They are grey with silvery flanks and white bellies. Pectoral fins are dark with bright yellow spots. Their diet is made of plants, seaweed, zooplankton and algae. They reproduce oviparously.

183. Spanish Dancer Nudibranch

Common name : Spanish dancer
Scientific name : Hexabranchus sanguineus
Family : Hexabranchidae
Native to : Indo-Pacific Ocean and the Red Sea
Interesting fact : Rhinopores are two horn-like sensory organs on the head that help these fish locate food or a mate.
Conservation status : Not Evaluated

The Spanish dancer nudibranch is a large, colourful sea slug living among coral reefs. They are over 40 cm long, have bright red mantles with golden gills and rhinopores. They crawl and swim feeding on sponges. These hermaphrodites lay brightly coloured eggs in spiral, ribbon-like mass on a solid substrate. Lifespan is less than a year.

184. Sperm Whale

Common name : Spermacet whale, Cachelot, Pot whale
Scientific name : Physeter macrocephalus
Family : Physeteridae
Native to : Oceans worldwide
Interesting fact : Sperm whales are called so due to the massive organ in the forehead containing 900 litres of spermaceti, a wax-like liquid used in echolocation.
Conservation status : Vulnerable

The sperm whale is the largest of the toothed whales growing up to 20.5 metres long and weighing up to 57,000 kg. They have large, block-shaped heads, S-shaped blowholes and cone-shaped teeth. They can dive up to 2,250 metres staying submerged for 90 minutes. They feed on squid and octopuses. Lifespan is 60 years.

185. Spotted Wobbegong Trout

Common name : Carpet shark, Spotted wobbegong
Scientific name : Orectolobus maculatus
Family : Orectolobidae
Native to : Indo-Pacific Ocean
Interesting fact : Wobbegong in Australian aboriginal language means 'shaggy beard' referring to the fleshy growth around the fish's mouth.
Conservation status : Near Threatened

The spotted wobbegong trout blends in with the sea floor with its carpet-like pattern on the skin. They live in coral, rocky reefs and sandy bottoms, growing up to 3.2 metres long. They feed on octopuses, crabs, lobsters, sea bass and luderick. They are ovoviparous; eggs are retained inside females in a brood chamber where they develop. Lifespan is 20-25 years.

186. Steelhead Trout

Common name : Rainbow trout, Kamloops
Scientific name : Oncorhynchus mykiss
Family : Salmonidae
Native to : Cold-water tributaries of the Pacific Ocean in Asia and North America
Interesting fact : They live most of their life in the sea and return to rivers for spawning.
Conservation status : Not Evaluated

The steelhead trout is dark-olive with a heavily speckled body and pink-red stripes along the side. They grow up to 120 cm long and weigh up to 25 kg. They feed on zooplankton, aquatic and terrestrial insects, molluscs, crustaceans, eggs of fish, minnows and small fish. They are popular as food in Western cuisine. Lifespan is 11 years.

187. Stellate Sturgeon

Common name : Star sturgeon
Scientific name : Acipenser stellatus
Family : Acipenseridae
Native to : Black, Azov,
Caspian and Aegean Sea basins
Interesting fact : It is anadromous,
living in the sea and migrating up rivers to spawn.
Conservation status : Critically Endangered
    Stellate sturgeons have slim, greyish-green or brown bodies with pale bellies. Their snouts are long, thin and straight with a row of five small barbells close to their mouths and 30-40 pale scales on the lateral line. This fish grows up to 220 cm long and weighs up to 80 kg. It feeds at night on fish, worms, crustaceans and molluscs. Its lifespan is 27 years.

188. Stonefish

Common name : Dornorn
Family : Synanceiidae
Native to : Indian and Pacific Oceans
Interesting fact : Stonefish can live out of water for 24 hours.
Conservation status : Not Evaluated
    The stonefish looks like a piece of stone with its hard brown surface and red, orange or yellow patches. It grows 30-40 cm long and weighs 2,400 gram. It has 13 venomous spines on the dorsal area, each with two venom sacs. The venom is injected when stepped on. It feeds on small fish, shrimp and crustaceans. Its lifespan is 5-10 years.

189. Striped Surgeonfish

Common name : Clown tang, Blue-banded surgeonfish, Clown surgeonfish, Zebra surgeonfish, Lined surgeonfish
Scientific name : Acanthurus lineatus
Family : Acanthuridae
Native to : Indo-Pacific Ocean
Conservation status : Least Concern
    The striped surgeonfish is a treat to the eyes with its alternating blue and yellow horizontal stripes. They live sin groups in shallow reef flats, slopes and gutters. It grows to 35 cm long and has a blade-like, venomous spine in the tail. They are herbivores, feeding on plankton and algae, sometimes on crustaceans. Lifespan is 10 years.

190. *Tassle Filefish*

Common name : Prickly leather-jacket, Tasselled leather-jacket, Leafy filefish
Scientific name : Chaetodermis pencilligerus
Family : Monacanthidae
Native to : Indo-Pacific Ocean
Interesting fact : The tassle filefish drifts with its head downward in an attempt to befool predators and prey.
Conservation status : Not Evaluated

The tassle filefish is well camouflaged with its laterally compressed body and horizontal light and dark stripes. The edges have dermal, tassle-like appendages that add to the camouflage. These fish live in lagoons and coastal areas with seagrass beds. It is a diurnal, solitary fish that grows up to 31 cm long. They are omnivores feeding on small fish, shrimp, invertebrates and algae.

191. *Teardrop Pufferfish*

Common name : Limespot butterflyfish, Yellow teardrop butterflyfish, Teardrop coralfish
Scientific name : Chaetodon unimaculatus
Family : Chaetodontidae
Native to : Indian Ocean
Interesting fact : They have fine, bristle-like teeth to feed on small organisms.
Conservation status : Least Concern

The teardrop pufferfish is a bright yellow and white fish with a tearing eyespot on the upper part of the body. They live in small groups, growing to 20 cm in length. It feeds on soft and hard corals, polychaetes, small crustaceans and filamentous algae. They are oviparous and form pairs during breeding. Lifespan is 5-7 years.

192. *Teira Batfish*

Common name : Longfin batfish, Longfin spadefish
Scientific name : Platax teira
Family : Ephippidae
Native to : Indo-West Pacific Ocean
Interesting fact : The teira batfish is a popular aquarium fish that is very peaceful and social.
Conservation status : Not Evaluated

Teira batfish have rounded, strongly compressed bodies with short, dark, vertical bars through the eyes and behind the operculum. They are yellow silver or dusky and grow to 27.5 inches long. Adults have bony humps on their foreheads. Spawning is in the open ocean. This omnivore feeds on plankton, sessile small invertebrates and marine algae. Lifespan is up to 5 years.

193. Textile Cone Snail

Common name : Cloth of gold cone
Scientific name : Conus textile
Family : Conidae
Native to : Indo-Pacific Ocean
Interesting fact : The conotoxin produced by them is extremely dangerous to humans.
Conservation status : Least Concern

The textile cone snail is a venomous sea snail that has a yellowish brown shell with longitudinal lines of brown, interrupted by triangular white spaces and a white aperture. It uses a radula to inject conotoxin to kill its prey. The tips of the proboscis have a harpoon-like radular tooth, capable of extending to any part of its own shell.

194. Thornback Skate

Scientific name : Raja clavata
Family : Rajidae
Native to : Australia, North-Eastern Atlantic and the Mediterranean
Interesting fact : The fish has a hole behind its eye called a spiracle to avoid silt getting into its gills.
Conservation status : Near Threatened

Thornback skates are bottom dwelling rays inhabiting mud, sand or gravel beds. They are 105-120 cm long and weigh 18 kg. It has a flattened, disc-shaped body, broad pectoral fins and a narrow, long tail. The upper surface and tail is covered with numerous thorns. They feed on fish, crustaceans and other bottom-dwelling creatures. Lifespan is 15 years.

195. Tiger Shark

Common name : Sea tiger
Scientific name : Galeocerdo cuvier
Family : Carcharhinidae
Native to : Tropical waters in the Southern Hemisphere
Interesting fact : The tiger-stripes fade with age.
Conservation status : Near Threatened

The tiger shark is known for its vertical tiger-stripes on its body. They grow up to 5 metres long and weigh 385-635 kg. They are solitary and nocturnal hunters, feeding mainly on squid, fish and turtles. They are ovoviviparous, mating once every three years and breed by internal fertilization, giving birth to 10-80 live pups. Lifespan is 12 years.

196. Tile Fish (Great Northern)

Common name : Great Northern tile fish,
Golden tile fish, Gunnet
Scientific name : Lopholatilus chamaeleonticeps
Family : Malacanthidae
Native to : Atlantic, Pacific and Indian Oceans
Conservation status : Least Concern

Tile fish live in self-made burrows in sandy areas near coral reefs. They grow 11–125 cm long and weigh up to 30 kg. Their yellow-brown or grey bodies are slender and elongated with long dorsal and anal fins. They feed on small benthic invertebrates, crustaceans, molluscs, worms, sea urchins and small fish. Their lifespan is 39-46 years.

197. Toad Fish (Dark)

Common name : Dark toad fish
Scientific name : Neophrynichthys latus
Family : Psychrolutidae
Native to : South-West Pacific, New Zealand.
Interesting fact : They can survive out of water for 24 hours.
Conservation status : Not Evaluated

Toad fish are found in marine, brackish and freshwater habitats. These bottom-dwellers are 7.5–57.0 cm long. They are heavy-bodied and scale-less with flattened heads and high-set eyes. They eat fish, sea worms, crustaceans and molluscs. The male uses the swim bladder as a sound-producing device to attract mates. Females produce sticky eggs, attaching them to the side of the nest. Its lifespan is 19 years.

198. Totoaba

Common name : Totuava
Scientific name : Totoaba macdonaldi
Family : Sciaenidae
Native to : Gulf of California in Mexico
Interesting fact : It migrates annually northward in winter to the Colorado River delta to spawn in spring.
Conservation status : Critically Endangered

The totoaba is dusky silver with darker fins. The body is elongated and compressed with a pointed head, large mouth and oblique lower jaw which is slightly projecting. It grows up to 2 metres long and weighs 100 kg. Sexual maturity is attained at 4-5 years of age. It feeds on fish and crustaceans. Lifespan is 25 years.

199. *Trumpet Fish*

Common name : Atlantic trumpet fish
Scientific name : Aulostomus maculatus
Family : Aulostomidae
Native to : Western Atlantic Ocean
Interesting fact : Trumpet fish change colour and stalk larger fish to hide and attack prey.
Conservation status : Not Evaluated

The trumpet fish lives in coral reefs or lagoons and can grow 40-80 cm long. Its long body is reddish-brown to greenish-yellow with an upturned mouth, small jaws and a long, tubular snout. It swims slowly and vertically, blending in with corals like sea pens, sea rods and pipe sponges. It feeds on small fish like wrasses and invertebrates.

200. *Tun Shell*

Common name : Giant tun
Scientific name : Tonna galea
Family : Tonnidae
Native to : Tropical seas worldwide
Interesting fact : Tun shell has a large foot with which it buries itself in the sand.
Conservation status : Not Evaluated

Tun shells are large marine snails inhabiting sandy or muddy bottoms in sea grass meadows. They have thin, strong shells and no operculum. The snail is larger than the shell which has a very large aperture and has spiralling ridges. They emerge at night to feed on echinoderms, crustaceans, bivalves, sea urchins and fish. Lifespan is 30 years.

201. *Turtle (Atlantic Ridley)*

Common name : Mexican ridley, Gulf ridley
Scientific name : Lepidochelys kempii
Family : Cheloniidae
Native to : Mexico, United States
Interesting fact : Sea turtles cannot retract their heads and limbs into their shells.
Conservation status : Critically Endangered

Seven species of sea turtles are known. They can grow 6-9 feet long, 3-5 feet wide and weigh up to 680 kg. They have an anaerobic system of energy metabolism as they are always ubmerged. Females return to the shore, dig holes and lay a clutch of 50-200 soft shell eggs. They feed on animals and plants. Lifespan is 80 years.

202. *Umbrella Shell*

Common name : Umbrella slug, Limpet
Scientific name : Umbraculum umbraculum
Family : Umbraculidae
Native to : Pacific and Indian Oceans
Interesting fact : The shell is too small for the animal to withdraw itself into it.
Conservation status : Not Evaluated

The umbrella shell is a sea slug attached to overgrown rock walls. An external shell, covered in algae, protects the gill plumes. The circular body is covered in pustules. This fish has two pairs of tentacles (situated close to the mouth) that are used for orientation. The middle part of the foot is used for locomotion. These fish feed on sponges.

203. *Unicorn Fish*

Common name : Bluespine unicorn fish, Short-nose unicorn fish, Unicorn tang
Scientific name : Naso unicornis
Family : Acanthuridae
Native to : Indian Ocean, Pacific Ocean and the Red Sea
Interesting fact : They have smooth skins and are less susceptible to skin diseases than other tangs.
Conservation status : Least Concern

Found in coral reefs and rocky areas is the unicorn fish that has a long, horn-like appendage on its forehead. They are greenish-grey with yellow dorsal and anal fins having blue lines. They use their sharp, scalpel-like tails as weapons in defence. These diurnal creatures feed on plankton and algae. Lifespan is 15 years.

204. *Vampire Squid*

Scientific name : Vampyroteuthis infernalis
Family : Vampyroteuthidae
Native to : Temperate and tropical oceans worldwide
Interesting fact : It is entirely covered in photophores, producing disorienting flashes of light lasting several minutes.
Conservation status : Not Evaluated

The vampire squid has a gelatinous, velvety jet-black body and large eyes that are red or blue. Its eight arms are connected by a webbing of skin, each arm lined with rows of spines and suckers on the tips. When threatened, it inverts its arms back over the body, presenting a larger body covered with spines. It feeds on copepods, prawns, cnidarians and detritus.

205. *Velvet Crab*

Common name : Devil crab, Witch crab, Velvet swimming crab, Lady crab
Scientific name : Necora puber
Family : Portunidae
Native to : North-West Europe
Conservation status : Not Evaluated

The velvet crab has a wide, flattened carapace that is blue, covered in reddish-brown hair, giving it a velvety texture. It has bright red eyes and ten narrow teeth between the eyes. It has velvety pincer of the same size that can deliver a painful nip. Adults feed on brown seaweeds, molluscs and crustaceans, while juveniles feed on small crabs and barnacles.

206. *Violet Sea Snail*

Common name : Common purple snail
Scientific name : Janthina janthina
Family : Janthinidae
Native to : Atlantic, Pacific and Indian Oceans
Interesting fact : It is a protandric hermaphrodite, born male and developing into female later.
Conservation status : Not Evaluated

This purple, floating snail has a long cylindrical snout, a paper thin shell, and lacks eyes and operculum. It agitates water with its foot, creating bubbles, binding them together with mucus and makes a raft to stay afloat on the ocean surface. If the bubble raft breaks, it will sink and die. It feeds on blue bottles and by-the-wind sailors.

207. *Viper Fish*

Common name : Sloan's viper fish, Sloan's fang fish
Scientific name : Chauliodus sloani
Family : Stomiidae
Native to : Tropical and temperate waters worldwide
Interesting fact : The first vertebra right behind the head acts as a shock absorber when it charges at its victim at a high speed.
Conservation status : Not Evaluated

The viper fish has large, sharp, fang-like teeth that almost reach its eyes. It is dark silvery blue in colour with a large mouth. It has a long dorsal spine tipped with a photophore that is used to attract prey. Spawning occurs throughout the year, with females releasing the eggs in open water to be fertilized. Lifespan is 30-40 years.

208. *Walrus*

Common name : Morse
Scientific name : Odobenus rosmarus
Family : Odobenidae
Native to : Arctic Ocean and sub-arctic seas of the Northern Hemisphere
Interesting fact : They can dive up to 80 metres and remain submerged for half an hour.
Conservation status : Data Deficient

    Walruses are large flippered marine mammals growing up to 2.2-3.6 metres long and weighing 800-1,700 kg. They are bulky animals with prominent tusks and whiskers. They feed on bivalve molluscs, shrimps, crabs, tube worms, soft corals and tunicates. Calves are born after a gestation period of 15-16 months. Lifespan is 20-30 years.

209. *Weedy Seadragon*

Common name : Common seadragon
Scientific name : Phyllopteryx taeniolatus
Family : Syngnathidae
Native to : Eastern Indian Ocean and South-Western Pacific Ocean
Interesting fact : The male has a brood pouch and cares for the developing eggs.
Conservation status : Near Threatened

    Living in rocky reefs, seaweed beds and seagrass meadows are these seadragons with small leaf-like appendages for camouflage and a number of short spines for protection. A long dorsal fin along the back and small pectoral fins on either sides of the neck provide balance. These fish feed on tiny crustaceans and zooplankton. Lifespan is 5-10 years.

210. *White-beaked Dolphin*

Scientific name : Lagenorhynchus albirostris
Family : Delphinidae
Native to : North Atlantic Ocean
Conservation status : Least Concern

    The white-beaked dolphin loves cold and sub-polar waters. It grows 230-310 cm long and weighs 180-350 kg. They have short, creamy white beaks, dark grey bodies with white patches and curved, sickle-shaped dorsal fins. They dive to feed on crustaceans, cephalopods and small schooling fish. A single calf is born after a gestation period of 11-12 months. Lifespan is 25 years.

211. White Shrimp

Common name : Grey shrimp, Lake shrimp
Scientific name : Litopenaeus setiferus
Family : Penaeidae
Native to : Atlantic Coast of North America and the Gulf of Mexico
Conservation status : Not Evaluated

The white shrimp is bluish white with a tinge of pink on the sides. They are 197 mm long with antennae that are three times the length of their bodies. It is an omnivore, feeding on seagrass and detritus. Spawning occurs in warm waters up to a depth of 9 metres within 9 km from the shoreline. Lifespan is 1-2 years.

212. Wreckfish

Common name : Atlantic wreckfish
Scientific name : Polyprion americanus
Family : Polyprionidae
Native to : Pacific, Atlantic and Indian Oceans
Conservation status : Data Deficient

Wreckfish inhabit rocky reefs, caves and shipwrecks. Their compressed bodies have small rough scales, scaly heads, spines on the dorsal fins and horizontal ridges on the opercles with short spines in the backs. They stay in schools of at least 5 and feed on crustaceans, mackerel, sand bass and whitefish. Lifespan is 60 years.

213. Wunderpus

Common name : Wonderpus octopus
Scientific name : Wunderpus photogenicus
Family : Octopodidae
Native to : Western Indo-Pacific Oceans
Interesting fact : The wunderpus can imitate other sea creatures in a flash to confuse predators and prey.
Conservation status : Not Evaluated

The wunderpus is an octopus with a unique pattern of white bars and spots over a reddish-brown mantle and long tentacles. It remains stationary, buried in sand with the eyes showing. It feeds on small fish, crabs and shrimps by grabbing them with its tentacles. Females spawn once and die after they have laid their eggs. Their lifespan is 2-3 years.

214. *Xiphias*

Common name : Swordfish, Broadbill
Scientific name : Xiphias gladius
Family : Xiphiidae
Native to : Atlantic, Pacific and Indian Oceans
Interesting fact : They are ectothermic animals
with special organs next to their eyes to heat their
eyes and brain, improving their vision.
Conservation status : Least Concern

Xiphias are migratory fish with elongated, round bodies, long, flat bills, losing all teeth and scales by adulthood. They grow up to 3 metres long and weigh 650 kg. They are solitaryre fish, feeding at night, rising to surface in search of squid, crustaceans, mackerels and barracudas. They spawn in warm waters during spring and summer. Lifespan is 9 years.

215. *X-ray Tetra*

Common name : Golden pristella tetra, Water goldfinch
Scientific name : Pristella maxillaris
Family : Characidae
Native to : South America
Interesting fact : It has an acute
sense of hearing.
Conservation status : Not Evaluated

The X-ray tetra has faint gold scales on a translucent layer of skin, allowing its backbone to be clearly seen. It returns to floodlands to spawn during rainy season, laying 300-400 eggs scattered amongst the vegetation. Fries hatch 24 hours later. It feeds on aquatic plants, worms, insecs, small crustaceans and insects' larvae. Lifespan is 3-4 years.

216. *Yellow Tang*

Common name : Yellow sailfin tang, Yellow surgeonfish
Scientific name : Zebrasoma flavescens
Family : Acanthuridae
Native to : Pacific and Indian Oceans
Interesting fact : It has sharp spines near the tail
which is used in defence and as an anchor
in the rocks.
Conservation status : Least Concern

The yellow tang is found in shallow reefs and grows up to 20 cm long. It has a bright yellow oval body that fades at night into a prominent brownish patch in the middle with a horizontal wide stripe. This herbivore feeds on plankton and algae. It provides cleaner service to sea turtles, removing algal growth from its shell. Lifespan is 30 years.

217. Yellow Tail Amberjack

Common name : Great amberjack, Silver king
Scientific name : Seriola lalandi
Family : Carangidae
Native to : Pacific and Indian Oceans
Conservation status : Not Evaluated
    The yellow tail amberjack is found
around offshore islands, rocky reefs and kelp beds.
It grows up to 250 cm long and weighs 52 kg.
It has a blue back, silvery white sides, a belly, a narrow bronze strip along the middle,
yellowish fins and a tail. It feeds on squid, crabs, smelts, mackerels, anchovies and
sardines. Its lifespan is 30 years.

218. Yeti Crab

Common name : Yeti lobster
Scientific name : Kiwa hirsute
Family : Kiwaidae
Native to : Pacific and Antarctic ridge
Conservation status : Not Evaluated
    The yeti crab is a hairy white crab
sensing its surroundings with its hair, as it
lacks eyes. The arms are covered in bacteria
that live and grow in the hair. These bacteria
are a source of food for the crab which also feeds on mussels, shrimp and algae. Males
prefer warmer waters and egg-carrying females and juveniles prefer the coldest waters.

219. Yellow Fin Tuna

Scientific name : Thunnus albacores
Family : Scombridae
Native to : Tropical and sub-tropical
oceans worldwide
Interesting fact : They are built for
speed, capable of capturing fast-moving baitfish like
flying fish and mackerels.
Conservation status : Near Threatened
    The yellow fin tuna has a very dark metallic blue body with a silvery belly having 20
vertical lines. The second dorsal fin, anal fin and tail are bright yellow. It travels in schools
with similar sized fish, sometimes schooling with other tuna species. It feeds on crustaceans,
squid and fish. Lifespan is 8 years.

220. Yellow Moray Eel

Common name : Green eel, Brown reef eel, Sydney green moray
Scientific name : Gymnothorax prasinus
Family : Muraenidae
Native to : South-West Pacific region
Interesting fact : It swims by flexing its whole body into lateral waves.
Conservation status : Not Evaluated

The yellowish-brown to green eel has an orange head and a yellow border around its tail, growing up to 4 feet in length. Their powerful jaws have sharp fang-like teeth and their tubed nostrils give them an excellent sense of smell. They are nocturnal staying in crevices and holes during the day. They feed on reefs, fish and crabs.

221. Zebra Shark

Common name : Leopard shark, Common carpet shark
Scientific name : Stegostoma fasciatum
Family : Stegostomatidae
Native to : Indo-Pacific Oceans
Interesting fact : Zebra sharks move like eels with their tails moving from side-to-side.
Conservation status : Vulnerable

Only the juveniles of the zebra shark have stripes whereas the adults have leopard-like spots. This fish has longitudinal ridges on its cylindrical body and a tail almost half its body-size. They live in sandy bottoms around coral reefs and feed on worms, molluscs, crustaceans, octopuses and small fish. They reproduce oviparously and have a 5-month gestation period.